This book stands out like a lion a⸍   t
tells the story of a true hero—one v   .t
in serving the ungrateful and lovin   ?-
giver manages to wrestle hope fron   's
insights are welcome and profound; her story is a stirring chapter in
God's grand story starring those who find power in weakness and true
joy in loving the least of these. Bless you!

Phil Callaway
Speaker, author of 25 books
editor of *Servant* magazine
syndicated columnist & radio host
www.philcallaway.ab.ca

As Bobbi first submitted her *The Reluctant Caregiver* manuscript to
me in installments, I eagerly awaited each set of chapters. Her sharp
eye for detail, her empathy for the unuttered, her honesty concerning
her faith and her own struggles, as well as her ability to find wry hu-
mour in circumstances that would have most people sobbing in de-
feat—all of these will give hope and inspiration to many, many read-
ers, particularly, but not necessarily, if they're living through a similar
situation. Through her living and writing of this story, Bobbi has been
blessed and become a blessing for others.

Rev. Patricia Anne Elford, OCT, BA, M Div
Pastor, editor, educator, public speaker
award-winning freelance writer

How do you give care to an aging parent who has wounded you in childhood and who continues to express her dislike of you to your face? Add to that, your parent's uncalled for and bitter accusations when you have gone out of your way to give help. Then add dementia to the mix. And how do you keep on doing all this in a way that would please God when you would rather run the other way?

Bobbi Junior's book, *The Reluctant Caregiver*, provides insight into how to help an aged and dependent parent, with or without dementia, in a respectful way. It also provides insight into how you can enter into God's grace to enable you to do the right thing for your parent, setting aside your own agenda, to discover God is also at work changing you.

I'm an avid reader, and I found her book, which I read in one sitting on two different occasions, as intriguing as any biography I've ever read (and I have over a hundred in my library). I could not put it down.

If laughter is a "medicine which does the heart good," you will find this a pill, which will tickle your funny bone with joy and encouragement.

Bobbi has been a faithful participant in our midweek prayer and bible study group. Our group has been privileged to walk with her in prayer as she encountered the many obstacles in this journey. It has given us much encouragement to pray with Bobbi and see God's miracles unfold. Needless to say, I highly recommend this biography.

Pastor Brad Olson
Richmond Park Church
Edmonton, Alberta

The RELUCTANT Caregiver

Navigating the Turmoil of the Sandwich Generation

Bobbi Junior

Printed in Canada

ISBN: 978-1-4866-0629-0

Word Alive Press
131 Cordite Road, Winnipeg, MB R3W 1S1
www.wordalivepress.ca

MIX
Paper from
responsible sources
FSC
www.fsc.org
FSC® C016245

Library and Archives Canada Cataloguing in Publication

Junior, Bobbi, 1951-, author
    The reluctant caregiver / Bobbi Junior.

Issued in print and electronic formats.
ISBN 978-1-4866-0629-0 (pbk.).--ISBN 978-1-4866-0630-6 (pdf).--
ISBN 978-1-4866-0631-3 (html).--ISBN 978-1-4866-0632-0 (epub)

    1. Junior, Bobbi, 1951- --Family. 2. Caregivers--Religious life.
3. Dementia--Patients--Care. 4. Care of the sick--Religious aspects--
Christianity. I. Title.

BV4910.9.J85 2014   248.8'619683   C2014-905709-1
                                                 C2014-905710-5

Dedicated to my brother, husband and children,
who never said, "You should…"

And to Jesus, who said "Let me."

Contents

Acknowledgements

When I began this project, I felt isolated in trying to write my story. As I look back, I can only acknowledge God's goodness when I recognize the many persons he brought in, each at just the right time, to play a role in bringing this book to fruition.

Meet some of them:

Jesus, who gave me the most meaningful content for the book, and brought me through the story.

Rick, my husband, whose support in Mom's care is never-ending and who understands my need to write about it.

Sheila Webster, who read the raw journal and let me know that, "Yes, this is a story to be told."

Patricia Anne Elford who edited patiently and taught me so much in the process.

Karin Preiss, who loved Mom through her mean times, and kept it up until Mom learned to love her in return. (*The sequel to this story.*)

Ruth Snyder and Sharon Espeseth, who diligently read and sent edits and suggestions.

My Millcreek Writers' Group who said, "Don't you dare leave it unfinished!" when I became tired of the project.

The Writers' Café, my second writers' group, who steadfastly encouraged me and with whom I share mutual learning.

Riet Scott, Tina Markeli, Randy Boettcher, Mary Harvey, Brad and Donna Olson, who each read the final draft and encouraged me to send it off.

Richmond Park Evangelical Missionary Church in Edmonton, who prayed me through the living and writing of my story.

InScribe Christian Writers Fellowship and The Word Guild Facebook groups who take all my questions seriously and answer them with thought and concern.

Alberta Caregivers Association and their Caregiver Ambassadors Workshops, where caregivers learn to tell their stories.

Others too numerous to mention have been part of this journey as well. May God bless all of you.

Foreword

The first time I heard Bobbi talk about her experience as a caregiver will stay with me forever. My organization had invited her to speak, to share some of her story, at an Edmonton event for Family Caregiver Week. That day, Bobbi talked about the struggles of taking her now disabled daughter home from the hospital after a devastating accident. It was a story about losing hope, about becoming so wrapped up in caring that she almost lost herself in the process. The room was spellbound. Years later, caregivers still ask about Bobbi. They want to know how she's doing; they tell me that her story changed their lives. Beyond the particulars of Bobbi's situation, there was an experience they could all relate to. She wasn't just telling her story, she was telling theirs as well.

The caregiving story is too often about being invisible. As a whole, society doesn't see caregivers. Doctors and nurses ask how the patient is doing. Well-meaning acquaintances inquire after your loved one's health, rather than your own. Ask a caregiver about their experience and there is a good chance they'll tell you about the care recipient's diagnosis, the care recipient's triumphs and struggles, and the care recipient's needs. Even in their own story, the caregiver is cast as a minor character.

Most people take on the role of caregiver—for their parents, their spouses, their children and friends—without a second thought.

This is someone they care about. They do it out of duty and they do it out of love. What is rarely realized is that providing care has an impact on the caregiver too. You watch someone you care about struggle and suffer. Your relationships change and friends fade away. You have to navigate a maze to find even the smallest supports. People tell you to 'look after yourself' but you just don't have the time.

It can be hard to ask for help or to admit a weakness. In our society, caregiving is thought to be a noble calling. You are being strong for your loved one. Your role is to quietly support them as they go through this difficult time. While you may be praised for how well you manage, there is rarely any recognition of how challenging caregiving can be. As a caregiver, you place these expectations on yourself, too. Asking for help is like admitting that you aren't a good enough daughter or husband or parent.

As a society, we don't talk openly about the realities of caregiving. There isn't a common understanding of the negative aspects of providing care. While feeling resentful, hopeless, frustrated, guilty, angry or sad is normal and should be expected, most caregivers have no idea others feel that way too. It can be incredibly lonely.

Bobbi's gift to the crowd when she spoke at Caregiver Week was to break the silence. It was saying that it's okay to have negative feelings. It was saying that it's okay to ask for help, that you aren't any less of a parent or a spouse or a child for needing support.

Bobbi's journey in this book reflects the lessons learned from her earlier caregiving experience. While there are still roadblocks, detours and frustrations, this is the story of learning to hold onto hope. It isn't easy. You have to let things go. You have to recognize and accept your limitations. You have to ask for help.

Just as important as setting boundaries is cultivating the things that give you hope. It may be having supportive friends and family, finding small rituals, treasuring a new or closer relationship with your care recipient, putting your faith in a higher power.

Caregiving will never be easy, but the experience can be treasured. There are individuals and organizations to help you along the way. And remember, on the caregiving journey you are never really alone.

God Bless,
Anna Mann
Executive Director,
Alberta Caregivers Association

The Alberta Caregivers Association was born out of the ashes of one caregiver's burnout. A group of caregivers saw the need for an organization that would focus on the caregiver, rather than the care recipient. In 2001, the Alberta Caregivers Association was formed. We support caregivers by providing one-on-one and group programs, by educating professionals, by raising awareness of caregivers in the general public and by advocating for policy changes. We envision an Alberta where all caregivers are valued and supported.

Visit us at
www.albertacaregivers.org

To the Reader:

This story is really the story of two journeys: my mother's with dementia, and mine with Jesus as I provided her care. Family members are an important part of the story but to preserve their privacy, several names have been changed.

Introduction

Divorced from my mother for more than forty years, my father periodically asks, "Why did your mother despise you?"

I wonder if he really wants to ask, "Why are you your mother's caregiver when she never cared for you?"

When I was a child, Mom was emotionally unavailable. At times she failed to protect me. In my teens, she turned her back on my struggles. Later, when my own child was seriously ill, she kept a safe distance. We remained polite but estranged.

Then, in 2011, Mom began to call on me to take her for groceries, help manage her banking, make and keep appointments. Over time I came to realize her requests were a grudging admission of a truth she was loath to accept: without help, she could no longer manage to function independently. The undiagnosed cause was dementia.

Her capacity diminished and my brother and I became the unwilling recipients of her paranoid fears as she ranted and accused us of elder abuse. Yet I kept going back, providing her care.

Why? Did I still seek my mother's approval, or was there something more?

For a year, my brother and I laboured to meet Mom's needs and fulfil her requests. For a year, I struggled with her demands, managing to meet them only when I set myself aside and relied on Jesus.

In the process, I learned the truth of 2 Corinthians 12:9: "My grace is sufficient for you, for my power is made perfect in weakness."

No Other Resource But You

Chapter One

Our mother may be ninety years old, but when she's in a fury, she's a force to be reckoned with. Or not, as the case may be. Hence, my brother's sudden departure.

He phones me on his cell from a truck stop café just outside of town.

"I know it's the dementia," he says in a tense voice, "but the things she was doing, saying…Her dementia doesn't mean I should let her get away with just anything."

"What set her off?"

"She locked me in the basement," he fumes. "Again. I told her yesterday she had to leave the deadbolt open when I'm sleeping down there. What if there's a fire? She seemed to grasp what I was saying. She even apologized. And I reminded her when I went down to bed last night— 'Don't lock the door.' But this morning it was locked again. I pounded on the door and called, but she didn't answer. Finally I just went back down, had a shower and packed my stuff. Then I sat and waited. She opened the door at ten."

"Did you ask her why she locked it?"

"Not really. If she couldn't tell me yesterday, why would she be able to today? I did tell her I wasn't staying any longer if this was how she was going to treat me. It's just not safe."

"You're right," I agree. "It's not." *Poor Lawrence. What a difficult position. Driving all this way in the middle of winter to visit our mother, and then this.*

"I did try to explain the safety factor again," he says. "But the discussion deteriorated really fast. She wouldn't see reason, and told me I could just get out if I was going to be that way. Like I was twelve years old or something! I wasn't going to stay another night anyway, not if I was going to be locked in again, so I grabbed my stuff and left."

I sigh. His own sigh echoes in my ear.

"I don't know what to do," I say, feeling as confused and helpless as Lawrence sounds.

"Neither do I," he replies. "If we had Power of Attorney we could take some action, but there's nothing we can do without Mom agreeing." I can hear him paying his bill as he prepares to leave the restaurant. "Maybe give her a call when she cools down," he adds, "and see if you can find out what was going on."

"I'll do that," I say and wish him safe travels.

We say goodbye and Lawrence drives the five hours back to his homestead in Northern Alberta, his intended weeklong visit having lasted just two nights.

I try to reach Mom by phone over the next few days, but with no success.

What to do?

Lord, when it comes to caring for Mom, I'm way out of my depth. All I can think to do is lay my confusion before you. I don't know how to pray. I don't know how to help. Every indication is that Mom's dementia is increasing. I know she needs help, but she insists on remaining independent. I want to do what's right in your eyes, but I don't know what the right thing is.

As I wrote these words in my journal, I had a sudden revelation.

That's exactly where you want me to be: not knowing what to do. Only then will I turn to you to fill my needs.

Psalm 145:15 entered my mind: "The eyes of all look to you, and you give them their food at the proper time."

When I was a child, I always knew Mom would provide meals for me. I didn't go to her during the day to remind her that I'd be hungry later. I didn't check to see if she had enough groceries. I didn't ask if she had a recipe ready. Over the years she had proven herself trustworthy in this. It didn't occur to me to doubt her provision.

If I could trust my mother for adequate provision, how much more could I trust Jesus? Had Jesus proven himself trustworthy? The answer was indisputable. Yes.

Jesus says, "Come to me, all you who are weary and burdened, and I will give you rest... For my yoke is easy and my burden is light" (Matthew 11:28, 30).

Lord, can I take you literally? Can I give you my concerns, quit thinking about all this and carry on with my life while I wait for you to direct me?

It seems that's what you're saying.

Okay then. This feels irresponsible, but so be it. I'm going to serve my mother with no resource other than you. You're the potter, I'm the clay. I'll show up at Mom's house when you lay it on my heart to visit, and I'll let you take charge when I get there. I place my mother and her needs in your hands.

I sat back from my prayer and relief washed over me. The contrast in my spirit was tangible. Until I let it go, I hadn't been aware that I'd been feeling such a heavy weight of responsibility for my mother. As I realized those cares had been cast on Jesus, my stress diminished like a balloon deflating.

The following days were filled with a wonderful sense of peace. I felt no urge to call or visit. I didn't fret. I wasn't trying to figure out Plan A, Plan B, and Plan C. True to his word, Jesus gave me a week filled with peace and rest.

Then came the day when Jesus said, "Go."

Chapter Two

I felt not so much a pull to contact Mom but rather a release. My day as Communications Coordinator for the Family Solutions Group ended at four. Back home, I dialed Mom's number and counted the rings. Eight, nine, ten. No answer. I called again that evening, then the next morning, and again at lunch. Something was wrong, of that I was sure.

Mid-afternoon I left work early and headed to Mom's house, questions swirling.

Is she angry and not answering the phone? Is she sick? Is she dead? If she's alive, what state of mind will she be in?

I had no idea what to expect.

Oh, God, I really don't want to do this!

As I drove the freshly plowed streets, I recalled a television commercial that was meant to illustrate the difficulties that come with dementia. The scene depicted a gently befuddled grandma and her adult son. The lady was putting lemons in odd places and wearing her coat in the house.

Perhaps that was true for some, but it sure wasn't our experience.

The closer I got to Mom's house, the more my anxiety increased. I prayed for wisdom, patience and understanding as I wound my way through the residential streets. I wasn't in any hurry. Given our rocky history, finding myself in this caregiver role was a stretch for both of us.

Mom had left our father when I was nineteen; she had lived alone in her house ever since. Fiercely private and independent, Mom had a modest social circle. By now, most relatives and friends had passed away. The few still living were in other provinces. By default, I'd become the only available support.

I managed to squeeze my car into a spot on the snow-rutted street. I climbed over the drifts in front of Mom's old bungalow. A shovelling service had cleared her sidewalk, but even so, I was sure she would never venture out in the snow and ice. She often told me how foolish it was for old people to go out in winter when they could fall and break a limb. The fear of being helpless was a constant demon that hovered on the periphery of Mom's world; she lived her life accordingly.

The mailbox, labeled "Nancy Bastion" in small letters, was empty. I was encouraged. She must be well enough to bring in the mail. I climbed the steps and knocked.

After a few moments I knocked again, then counted to thirty, poised to hear her unlatch the door. Thirty seconds felt like a long, long time as I stood there shivering in the cold.

Mom is so deaf. Is she simply not hearing? Is she refusing to answer? Anything could be going on.

I knocked a third time, really hard, and waited another thirty seconds.

Nothing.

The key Mom had given me several years before would unlock her back door.

Wondering if she would remember she had given me a key, I went around back and opened the screen door.

Will she assume it's me? Or will she think it's a burglar and panic?

Given the dementia, I couldn't be sure what to expect. Our fragile relationship didn't boast any foundation that gave me the right to do what I was about to do.

I did it anyway.

Unlocking the door, I stepped into the dark porch. Hesitantly, I called out, "Mom? Hi! It's me. Hello?" I crept up the two steps and tiptoed into the kitchen, not sure what I'd find.

The light was on. The 1940's grey Arborite counter was fairly tidy. A used teacup and an empty glass jar sat on the cutting board. Several quart jars of water lined the backsplash, but this was normal. "You never know when the water might go off." The porcelain sink, dull after decades of scrubbing with Comet, the foaming cleanser, was empty. Everything appeared as it should. I stepped farther into the kitchen. The glow of Mom's bedroom light spilled into the hallway. Calling out again, I peeked around the corner into her room.

Mom sat on the far side of the bed. Shrunken now, she weighed no more than ninety-five pounds. Her curved spine had twisted her body a little off-centre, causing her to lead with one shoulder. We made eye contact—her face registering outrage at my intrusion—and I took in the picture of this waif-like woman, dressed in a faded skirt and pastel smock. I noted slouched socks with the ankle bands cut off, her way of ensuring they wouldn't be tight on her legs.

Her blankets were straightened, but the pillow was askew. Strewn on the quilt was a confusion of papers—bank statements, bills, junk mail, articles and ads cut from the newspaper. A small pile of change was scattered near her hip.

She glared at me, incensed, and quickly looked away. "What are you doing here?" she demanded.

"I came to see you. I've been phoning but there was no answer."

"Why would I bother? What do I want that for?" Spittle showed at the corner of her mouth. She wiped it hard with her hand.

"Mom, are you okay?"

"Of course I'm not okay. You know that! Why would you even ask?"

"Has something happened?"

"This!" She indicated the pile of quarters, nickels and dimes, picked some of it up and gave it a weak, overhand toss. The coins scattered a little farther. "They want money. They call and call for money. Just give them this. Just give it to them!"

"Are telemarketers calling you?"

"Just give it to them. What do they know? They want money for the airport. I don't want it. Give it to them."

I didn't know how to respond. All I could think to do was reflect what I saw. "You're really upset," I said simply.

"Why was that man here?" she suddenly demanded. Now, tears glistened in her eyes.

"Was there a man here?" This didn't sound good.

"Yes," she burst out. "He hid in the basement. I didn't sleep for nights because I knew he was there." Tears spilled, and her voice shook with the rage of helplessness.

"Mom, Lawrence was here. Your son. He was here last week. He slept in the basement."

"Your brother! He thinks he can do anything. I finally sent him away."

"Yes, he told me he left." Again, I was at a loss. I didn't want to try to direct the conversation. Was there something she needed to tell me? All I could do was keep listening and try to weave the threads of what she was saying into something I could understand.

The exchange went on for an hour. I knelt on the floor by the bed as Mom sat on its edge, fuming and ranting. Bit by bit I was able to decode some of what was going on in her mind. It seemed that when Lawrence went to the basement to sleep, she was aware there was a man down there, but couldn't remember who he was. This was very frightening, especially at night, so of course she had locked the door to the basement so this man couldn't come up into her space. Even then, she had been afraid that he might break down the door.

Scattered through her rambling description, she frequently mentioned "wallet" and "keys."

"I hid them," she suddenly announced with renewed tears and a gut-level sob. "I knew he might want them, so I hid them. Now I have no money. I can't go anywhere. How can I eat?" She wailed in anguish.

"Are you saying you hid your keys and wallet and now you can't find them?"

"How do you get food if you have no money? You have to have money!"

I worked to resist reasoning with her. Logically, we could go to the bank and get more cash, but I knew that wasn't the point. The point was that her brain was sabotaging her ability to remain independent, and that thought horrified her. The point was that if she couldn't find her keys and her money, she might have to admit the deterioration in her brain was winning the war—a war her intelligence and ingenuity were still determined to win.

"This has been a really upsetting week for you," I repeated.

Through more circuitous conversation I came to understand that after Lawrence had left, Mom had forgotten I was available to help out. She believed she was on her own. Without her keys or wallet, she was sure she was going to starve to death, all alone, in her house. This independent, retired teacher now believed she was helpless in every sense of the word. She was terrified and humiliated.

Mom continued to ramble, storming through semi-related topics, but the fight was going out of her. It seemed the fear was dissipating, too. Gradually she began to remember that I was one who could help. She started making eye contact and seemed to become mindful of the fact that she wasn't alone.

Unexpectedly, she rose from the bed. Following her lead, I got up too, grateful to straighten my aching knees. She continued to mutter as her feet, apparently of their own accord, took her to the dresser. I followed quietly.

Still murmuring, her blue-veined hands opened the top drawer. Twisted fingers took out a package wrapped in an embroidered handkerchief. Commenting on nothing in particular, her hands unwrapped the hanky to uncover a satin jewelry bag. Tucked in the bag was a small plastic case. Mom continued to talk as she unpeeled more layers. Finally, the last layer was folded back. Revealed in her hand was her precious black wallet. In the wallet were her keys and cash.

I blinked with surprise and put my hand on her arm. Her skin felt fragile and insubstantial. Unsure how best to respond, I opted for a positive spin. "Look at that," I said. "You hid your things so well that even you couldn't find them at first. But now, here they are!"

Mom stared at the wallet and keys and then slumped, grasping the dresser for balance. "I can't believe it," she said, shaking. "I can't believe it. I feel like I'm going to faint. How could I do that? How could I do something like that?"

My heart ached for her. Now that the panic was gone and her mind was functioning again, she could recognize how erratically she had behaved. Even with dementia, Mom had the ability to step back to view herself from a distance and critically analyze her behaviour. This time what she saw appeared to be worse than the harrowing week through which she'd lived. Relief and shame seemed to battle for control.

I decided normalcy was the best medicine at this point. "I think this calls for tea and cookies. How about you?"

Mom seemed grateful to have a way back into her ordinary routine. She followed me to the kitchen and watched from the table as I made mugs of tea. We sat and chatted awhile longer. Mom guzzled her tea and I poured her a second. She downed the cookies as if she were half starved. I wondered if she'd even been able to feed herself during this week of mental chaos.

Periodically Mom's conversation returned to the fact that she had hidden and lost her most precious possessions: her wallet, containing her means of providing for herself, and her keys, symbols of her control over her environment.

As I made my way home a little later, I asked Jesus: *Is this a turning point in Mom's life? It's clear she's in a precarious position. How do we move forward? It makes sense to visit often to make sure she has meals and is grounded in reality. But, will she allow it now that the crisis is over?*

You're my resource, Jesus. You led me through today. I'm waiting on you for tomorrow.

Home Care

fter such a distressing week, I felt it was important to stay in close contact with Mom, at least for a while. At the same time, I didn't want to make it obvious. If she thought I was trying to usurp her independence, she might shut me out again.

Each day I came up with a fresh excuse to invite myself over.

"I'm picking up some groceries after work. Can I drop by for tea?"

Or, "Rick's working tonight so I thought I'd come by with some soup for us to share." At the mention of my husband, Mom always smiled and asked if he was coming too. Rick was one of the few people Mom had always trusted, and his infinite patience was a calming influence on her. Unfortunately he worked the two-to-midnight shift, so on weekdays, Mom had to settle for my persistent company.

Dementia notwithstanding, Mom knew what I was doing, and for a while she allowed it. I think she understood that retreating from outside contact in the week after her altercation with Lawrence had nearly put her over the edge. For a few days Mom graciously tolerated my presence, but only until she could come up with a plan. Human contact and regular meals gave her the nourishment and stability she needed to do some thinking.

Snow was swirling through the streets on this bitter Tuesday. Inside, we shared a dinner of buttered toast with baked chicken and well-cooked, easy-to-chew broccoli. As we ate, Mom casually broached her idea.

"People come in and help seniors. They come and you pay them," she said.

It took me a moment to decode her meaning. "Are you talking about home care?"

She nodded sagely.

This wasn't new. In the past, she'd mentioned this as something she would do "when the time comes." She'd read up on home care services while her brain was still strong, so the concept was firmly established in her mind.

I wondered if she would follow through. I felt a guilty flutter of hope. It would be such a relief to share the responsibility for Mom's well-being with someone else.

I recalled a lesson she'd repeated often during my childhood: "If you need something, do it yourself, or hire someone to do it. Never let yourself be obligated to relatives!"

When I first started taking Mom for groceries she'd paid me twenty dollars a trip. "For your gas," she'd explain. As time went on she often forgot, but it was always her intention to pay me. "Don't let me forget to give you some money," she'd say as we left the grocery store. If she remembered, I would take it, as I knew it helped her feel self-sufficient. If she forgot, I 'forgot' too.

"So you're thinking about home care," I said as I poured us each a cup of tea. "What do you have in mind?"

"I could get someone to come to the house a few times a week. Tuesday and Thursday. Tuesday? Wednesday? And help with laundry. They can carry the basket downstairs. They can carry it. I could fall on the stairs carrying a basket."

I nodded in agreement, but her eyes focused somewhere behind me. She appeared to be working to search for the words she'd practised in her mind. Verbalizing them took great concentration.

"And cleaning . . . washing a floor. Who can? And I could talk," she suddenly said in a rush. "I don't ever see anyone. They could talk."

Loneliness. Even an introvert needs some human contact. Trapped by winter, Mom's enforced isolation must have been overwhelming at times.

"That sounds like an excellent plan," I agreed.

Red-rimmed eyes fixed on mine, and took on a determined look. She reached across the table to several neat piles comprised of random papers, envelopes, bills and flyers, along with scraps of notes written to herself. She shuffled through one, then another, tidied those two, and turned to a third.

Lord, give me patience. Help me refrain from hurrying her along.

Eventually Mom located an ad cut from the *Edmonton Seniors* newspaper.

"See? Care to You," she read out loud, "the company to call for all your home care needs. Our friendly staff will do laundry, cleaning, or provide companionship.' They give medicine too. I don't need medicine. They can carry the basket. Even groceries. Do you think she would drive me? Here—look at it."

Mom left me to read the ad while she went to the washroom. I scanned the scraps of notes that had escaped the piles, each with a few words written on them.

One said, "I'm a senior and I'm looking for some help in my home."

On the back of an envelope I read, "I'm a senior and I want someone to come and help me here."

The third changed it a bit. "I am calling about your ad. I'm a senior and I would like to meet."

Mom rejoined me and I asked, "Have you called this company?"

"I thought to," she responded.

"Would you like me to call and get some information?"

"Oh, yes. Yes. You could do that," she agreed enthusiastically.

It wasn't quite five o'clock, and the ad said they were open until six. I phoned right away. *Please, Lord, let me set something up quickly before Mom loses her momentum.*

I was encouraged by the professional who took my call. She answered as many questions as I could think to ask. As we talked, I jotted the answers on a notepad for Mom to review.

I'm not sure who was more excited, Mom or me. Over another mug of tea I explained that they charged by the hour, and required a minimum three hours at a time. She could tell them exactly what services she would require, and decide on the frequency of their visits. Mom sat without comment and listened carefully.

"Does that sound? Anyway?" she asked. Needing to concentrate was impeding her ability to formulate sentences.

"Yes, from what I've heard, those are the going rates. And three-hour shifts are pretty much the average." I hoped I was understanding her question correctly.

"Money is. We do know you know." Mom's brain was getting overwhelmed with all the information, so I took the next logical step.

"Do you want me to set up a meeting with them?" I asked.

"Oh yes. It's just a time. There's always a time."

"Would you like me to be here when they come to see you?"

"No," she said firmly. "I know you like to be in on these things. No. This is me."

Well, that was clear.

I called Care to You again and arranged an intake meeting for the next day.

"A lady named Adele will come to see you tomorrow at 10:00 a.m." I wrote it clearly on a clean sheet of paper.

"CARE TO YOU. Meeting Wednesday 10:00 a.m. Adele will come to Nancy's house."

Mom read it a couple of times, smiled and nodded.

Together we cleaned up the dishes.

"That was a good dinner," I said warmly. I zipped my coat to my chin and wrapped my scarf snuggly around my neck and face.

"I have enough food for tomorrow," Mom announced as we got to the door. "You don't have to come tomorrow."

"Okay," I agreed, thrilled that I would be able to go straight home from work and relax. "But will you phone me and let me know how the meeting goes?"

"Yes. I'll phone you tomorrow. Thanks for all your help." Mom reached up and gave me a hug.

"You're most welcome," I hugged her back, feeling the twist in her spine, and her gaunt frame under a worn blouse, now two sizes too big.

Mom stood at the door and watched until I had maneuvered the car onto the street. We both waved as I pulled away. I breathed a sigh of relief. Working full time and then spending time with Mom every day was not something I could keep up much longer.

The rearview mirror reflected the delighted grin lighting my face. I smiled at the other drivers inching along the icy roads in rush-hour traffic.

This is great, Lord. Mom will have regular home care support. I won't be her only line of defence. I want to be obedient to you and serve Mom according to her needs, but I didn't realize how burdened I've been feeling. Thank you for this solution. Please let everything go according to Mom's plan. I lay it all on you.

The next day I took great pleasure in driving straight home after work. There were errands I should have attended to, but I hung around the house instead, waiting for Mom to call and tell me how the meeting had gone.

At nine o'clock, discouraged, I got ready for bed.

The next evening I called Mom myself, ostensibly to set a date for grocery shopping. I didn't bring up the topic of home care, and neither did she. Like a skittish fawn, I didn't want to push her for fear she would bolt from the plan. I was determined to let things unfold in Mom's time.

The following day I picked her up after work. At Smitty's we shared an omelet and hash browns. No mention was made about Care to You.

After dinner we drove to the neighbourhood Safeway.

"Let me get the cart," she said, digging in her wallet. "Is it a quarter?"

"Yes, it's a quarter." I repressed a sigh. I had shown her many times how to put the coin into the slot on the handle of the cart, then to insert the key on the end of the chain, thereby releasing the cart, but she could never grasp it. Still, every time we shopped, she felt the need to try again.

"I have to be able to do this when I shop on my own," she said. "You're not always going to be with me."

I held my tongue. It seemed obvious to me, if not to her, that she would never shop for a cart full of groceries on her own again. Carrying out the futile lesson was easier than arguing, though.

Tucking Mom's arm through mine, we made our way across icy ruts to the cart corral. Once again I talked her through the procedure, guiding her hand a few times. The key popped loose and Mom tugged at the handle ineffectually. I added my strength, careful not to knock her over as the cart broke free. Together we rattled over the rough parking lot until we reached the automatic door. Glass panels slid apart, welcoming us with a blast of warmth and a puddled floor. We took our gloves off, loosened our scarves, and set about our task.

Shopping had become a well-rehearsed routine and we each slipped into our roles.

Mom took charge of the cart. I followed as she began in the produce section. Holding her list, she went directly to the bananas. A short inspection, and two were chosen.

"Do you need any lemon juice?"

She glanced over at the little yellow bottles. I'd learned that even with a list, Mom became confused. It was now my habit to ask "Do you need this?" or "Are you running low on that?" as we came to each of the items she liked to keep on hand. We were a well-oiled shopping machine by now.

"I'm so slow," she said by way of apology. She always said this.

I gave my usual response. "No problem." I have nothing planned this evening. We can take our time."

"Aren't you getting anything?" This was another predictable comment. It was important to her that I was shopping for myself as well. It couldn't appear I was doing her a favour.

"I need some coffee and Rick wants some baked beans. They're farther down." I always picked up a few things whether I needed them or not.

When we got to the bakery we added a cinnamon bun with cream cheese icing to the cart. Sharing some tea and a sticky treat after shopping was part of Mom's way of thanking me. As much as my waistline didn't need the sticky bun, the Lord had made it clear I was to be gracious and accept her hospitality. Consequently, at every shopping trip, I made sure to ask, "Do you want to get a treat?" She always did.

Once home, we exited the car and met at the trunk. Carefully I chose the lighter grocery bags for Mom to carry. Just as carefully she waited, eyeing the bags I chose for myself.

"Are you sure you aren't carrying too many? You'll hurt yourself. Give some more to me."

This little argument always played out as the next-to-last scene in *Getting Groceries*.

"Everything inside the porch," Mom insisted. "Leave things where they are. I will put them away later."

Following orders, I left the bags by the front door, searching until I found our calorie-laden snack. Tea and sticky bun was the final scene. Mom set out plates and I plugged in the kettle.

As tea steeped in our individual mugs, I noticed the ad from Care to You was still sitting on the table. Casually, I reached over and turned it to face Mom.

"So, did you meet with the lady from this place?" I asked.

"No," she mumbled. "Maybe she didn't come. Or I didn't hear the door. I could have been downstairs doing laundry."

My heart sank. I tried not to sigh audibly, but my disappointment was greater than I'd expected.

Didn't hear the door? Downstairs doing laundry? Mom, when you're expecting company, you're always dressed and hovering at the window for at least an hour ahead of time. You can't help yourself.

Dredging up a shred of hope I asked, "Do you want to set up another appointment then?"

"No." Her voice was firm this time. "You have to get things done anyway. It just takes a while."

Thinking about home care was something Mom could do but the reality of managing such a professional relationship must have been too much.

As I drove home, tears blurred my eyes.

⟡

That evening I wrote in my journal.

So we're back to the status quo, Lord. Mom has needs and I'm the need-filler. You've asked me to serve and I want to do that in a way that honours you. Forgive me for being grumpy and resentful at times. I feel so inadequate. It's harder because neither Mom nor I wants this kind of relationship. You know we were never close in the past. We spent most of our years avoiding each other. Being forced together now seems artificial.

Dear Lord, I feel like I'm living a lie.

Every time I know I'm to see her, anxiety builds. When I'm with her I feel like I have to be "on," to perform in a way that will be right for her. It drains the life out of me.

As Mom's daughter, I really don't want to be doing this. But as your daughter, for you, I will.

This morning I read in 2 Samuel 24:22 that King David said he wouldn't offer burnt offerings to the Lord of that which cost him nothing.

Obedience comes at a cost.

You and I have been through this before, Jesus. I'm supposed to cast my cares on you and rest. If I could somehow set myself aside and let you work through me, would the anxiety go away? Should I feel loving emotions as I serve Mom in your name? Am I doing something wrong that's causing me to feel resentment, to feel like I can't keep this up?

But then, I think of the cost you paid to be obedient to your father on my account.

On my account!

Jesus, I pray that in my weakness you will reveal yourself to Mom. And to me.

Chapter Four

"*I*t sure is chilly out there." I struggled to get my coat off. My fingers tried to grasp the zipper as Mom clamped onto my arm with a claw-like grip and hustled me through the living room and into the kitchen.

"I was coming upstairs." She gestured to the three steps leading from her kitchen door to the back porch. On the left, more stairs continued from the porch down to the basement. Her knobby fingers gripped my arm. "Yesterday."

I nodded, shrugging my free arm out of its sleeve. "Shall I put the kettle on?"

"I did my laundry and I was coming up the stairs. Here." Releasing me, she marched with short, determined steps, elbows akimbo, eyeing the stairs warily. "Right here," she accused the risers. "How many times have I come up those stairs? I don't even remember falling," she said, astonishment in her voice.

"You don't remember..." It took a moment for her words to register. "You fell?" Unnoticed, my coat slid to the floor.

How could Mom fall? She's a walking safety campaign.

I thought about the chunks of foam she had fastened with masking tape to the ends of the stair railings. She'd explained, "I didn't know why my elbows were bruised all the time. I was bumping the railings."

I glanced at neon green Sticky-Notes garishly adorning the edge of the kitchen counter, orange ones climbing up the door frame to the hall. When they'd first appeared, I'd thought it was evidence of Mom's instability. It had turned out to be the opposite.

We were at the mall the day I'd made the connection. When I walked on Mom's right, we walked together well. If I walked on her left, she veered into me. I didn't know if it was loss of peripheral vision or some other cause, but the Sticky-Note system suddenly made sense. Little neon flags helped her notice corners and edges, preventing the bruises that took so long to heal.

Mom is smart, creative and determined. "Old people can be so stupid," she's said at times. "They ask for trouble. Get yourself hurt and you can't stay in your house anymore."

Mom's logic was impeccable. Bangs and bruises cause injury. Injured old folk are forced to leave their homes. Sticky-Note flags and foam-covered railings are proactive—a logical strategy once the reasoning is clear.

Together we turned our eyes to the offending steps. Both of us scowled at their silent betrayal.

Mom's explanation tumbled out, surprisingly clear and coherent.

"I was coming up the steps and all of a sudden I was lying in the middle of the kitchen floor, just staring at the ceiling. I wasn't hurt. I was just there."

Staring at the ceiling? How did you land on your back? No, best to let that go. Priorities first.

"You're sure you're okay?" I had to double-check, although she'd already made it clear. She furrowed her brow, warning me not to go further. There would be no discussion of old people needing to leave their homes. However, there would be discussion; Mom had been strategizing.

"I need an emergency plan." She led the way to the table. "So I don't lie there dying or something. Here—look at this." She pulled over the *Edmonton Seniors* paper, folded open to a half-page coloured advertisement: a smiling, perfectly coiffed, grey-haired woman displayed her arm, prominently accessorized by a black wristband. On the band was a large white button with black lettering against a red cross: *Emergency Alert.*

"See this?" Mom jabbed the page with a broken fingernail. "If I had one of these I could call for help. I would be on the floor and call for help. You just push the button. It stays on your wrist. See the picture?"

"I've heard of these." I joined in with enthusiasm, "My friend got one for her mom. The company came and hooked up the receiver to their phone and showed her how to work it. Would you like to see about getting one?"

"I don't know how much it would cost. How much would it cost? Do they come when you push the button? Who comes?" Explaining the details so Mom would understand seemed a little daunting, but I wasn't going to let this opportunity pass.

Lord, the home care plan didn't work, but maybe this one will. Please give me the right words.

"The company attaches a speaker and receiver to your phone." I paused, giving Mom time to think that through. "If you push the button on your wrist, a dispatcher responds through the speaker. If you don't answer, they call your emergency contact."

"They call me?"

"No. They speak to you. Through the speaker. My friend's mom pushed the button to see what would happen," I explained. "The dispatcher responded through the speaker and said, 'This is Alert Force. Do you need help?' And my friend's mom said, 'No. I was just testing the button.' The dispatcher said, 'Have a good day then.' But if my friend's mom hadn't responded, they would have sent help."

Mom listened intently, nodding.

Even though it was Mom's idea, I found myself selling the plan with the energy of a salesman.

That guilty flutter of hope was tickling my senses again. Even so, a contradictory voice whispered in my ear: *This could die the same death as the home care plan.*

I was having none of that.

I refuse to be pessimistic. Mom needs a way to be safe, and an Alert Button could give her that control. Jesus? Can you help make this work? If home care isn't feasible, maybe this is.

We discussed the details for a good half hour.

Mom seemed aware of what would be required, even repeating back scenarios I described.

"In the bathroom. They would hear the button," she stated.

"It would notify the dispatcher. Yes."

"In the basement? I do laundry."

"In the basement, too. It has a range that goes anywhere in the house."

"I push the button. They come."

"Probably I would come." I slowed things down and explained again. "They'd call your emergency contact first. If I wasn't available they'd send other help."

"How can you come? You work."

"I would leave work and come to check on you. My boss is fine with that."

I reached for the ad again. "It says the company is only open during work hours. How about we get Lawrence to take you there next time he's in town and they can tell you more about it?"

It also says they could send a technician right to the house, but we've tried that before. I'm not taking any chance of a repeat performance of the home care debacle. Perhaps a different approach will be more successful.

Later that evening, I called Lawrence and explained Mom's plan.

"When can you come down?" I asked.

"Is the weekend after next okay? I'll leave Wednesday morning. Should be in around one."

"Perfect." I gave him the company's phone number. "I think this is going to work," I said, nodding enthusiastically.

"We'll see." Lawrence was more cautious. "I'll call a few days before I come and make an appointment."

"Thanks, Lawrence. You're a good son to her. See you then!"

Once again, Mom had a plan. It was our job to facilitate carrying it out. There seemed to be a pattern developing. Mom's mind would latch onto something she had thought about and researched when her brain was still strong. Now, when she looked at the same ads, those memories were revived. With our help, she was ready to jump in with both feet. I hoped she didn't trip again in the process.

Lawrence called me from his cell phone when he arrived. We chatted optimistically for a few moments before Lawrence sighed.

"Do you think we're holding onto a hope that isn't tied to reality?"

"Perhaps," I replied.

He muttered something I didn't catch, followed by another sigh. "But this is our mother's plan," he stated. "We may be in our sixties, but we're still her children. She speaks. We obey."

"Crazy, isn't it? Do you think we'll get to a stage where we'll refuse to help her carry out these plans?"

"Maybe," he replied. "But as long as it seems feasible, I guess we carry on."

Lawrence wasn't able to get an appointment until the day before he had to leave. He called me Friday evening.

"All done" he announced. "We went to Alert Force and listened to their spiel. I don't know how much Mom was taking in. They explained it to her, but she seemed to shut down when they started talking. The guy asked to book a time for the technician to come and install it. She suddenly woke up and was not happy. She refused to have some stranger come to her house. I asked the guy to show me the system and it was pretty straightforward. We paid the fee and brought the equipment home and I set it up myself. So yeah, it's all in place!"

"Well, praise God!" I said to my non-believing brother.

"Praise God is right!" he responded in a surprisingly respectful tone.

Since the Alert Button was Mom's idea, we rested in the confidence that she too was pleased.

The next morning—Saturday—Lawrence left for his five-hour drive home. I carried on with my weekend, assuming all was well.

On Monday I headed to Mom's to take her for groceries. I was looking forward to seeing the Alert Force system in action. As I drove there, I prayed, *Lord, this emergency call button is most reassuring. Thank you for helping us to get it set up.*

Mom met me at the front door, muttering as I took off my boots. The living room was dark, curtains pulled. She hurried me through the gloomy room and into the kitchen. Dramatically she turned her back to the living room doorway.

Once again I was struck by the fact that when Mom is upset, she has no trouble finding her words. This was evident as she paced back and forth and unleashed a tirade.

"What did he do that for?" she shouted. "Look! All those wires all over the place." She waved her arms as though to banish demons lurking in the darkened room behind her. "I'm going to fall if I go in there. And someone's listening. They talked! I heard them." She lowered her voice and tucked in her chin. Her eyes were red-rimmed slits. "They're listening to everything I do. Can they see me? I have the lights off so they can't see me."

"Mom, sit down with me. Let me explain how it works."

She glanced furtively at the living room, but joined me at the kitchen table.

"Remember I told you that if you push the button on the wrist band, the dispatcher will call through the speaker to see if you're okay?"

Mom stared at the black band with the shiny white button, emblazoned with the international symbol of medical aid. She raised her wrist as though it were diseased. "This is what they're doing it from? This?"

"Yes." I tried to adopt a calm, matter-of-fact tone. "That's the button that alerts the dispatcher. Then she calls through the speaker to see if you're all right."

"What business is it of theirs if I'm all right? That's nobody's business but mine. If I want to die on the floor, that's my business. And keeping me out of my own living room!"

It might have seemed logical to repeat the explanation, but inside I felt a release. *Dear Lord. I'm not going to reason Mom past this hurdle, am I? The anger and confusion are bad enough.* But to be afraid of her own living room? That's more than anyone should have to put up with. *What do I do, Lord?*

Without conscious thought, the solution was there on the tip of my tongue.

"Do you want me to get rid of it?" I asked firmly. "I can pack it all up right now and get rid of it. Then you won't have to worry about it any more."

"Well, of course I want you to get rid of it. I don't know what you were thinking in the first place. Whatever possessed you?"

I glanced at the copy of the *Edmonton Seniors* on her table, still open to the ad with the smiling lady, wrist band raised in a confident salute. My bubble of hope fizzled to nothing.

What possessed us? Could I tell her that, to be honest, it was the hope that I wouldn't be solely responsible for Mom's well-being? Of course not—not without forcing her to confront her growing vulnerability as her mind struggled to make sense out of what used to be humdrum routine.

There was no acceptable answer to her question. I turned on the lamp in the living room, disconnected the wires and dismantled the speaker. Mom watched from a distance, safe within the confines of her well-lit kitchen. I wrapped everything up and stowed the offending items in the Alert Force box still sitting, untouched, on the couch.

I pointed to the wristband. "I'll put that in the box too."

"This?" she questioned, calmer now, but confused again. "They said I'm not supposed to take it off. What if I fall?"

What? What if you fall?

Resisting the desire to roll my eyes, I gritted my teeth.

Your words, Lord. Give me your words.

"I think the wristband has to go in the box too," I said, as though to a child. "Shall we put it in with the other stuff and see if it's okay there?" It wasn't a logical argument, but it was all I had to offer.

"Well…" she muttered, still hesitating.

I wasn't about to tackle her to get the wristband, but a small part of me considered it.

Jesus, what will convince her? Please! Before I lose my patience.

Oh, yes. Thank you! Mom follows rules to the letter. Not doing so is akin to rebellion.

"I think the company insists that the wristband stays with the wires and speaker. Should we try that and see if it's okay?"

With childlike compliance, Mom held her arm out towards me. Quickly unbuckling the clasp, I tucked the relinquished band in with rest of the equipment. Placing the box on the floor, I nudged my coat over it.

"Do you have a grocery list?" I asked, changing the subject.

Mom immediately began shuffling through the papers on her table. She'd been in such a state that, for once, she hadn't started a list. Together we checked the fridge and cupboards to see what was low. After some confusion about what to wear, we were ready to go.

Mom climbed awkwardly into the car, her foot trying to step onto the seat instead of the floor. Perhaps the stress of the last few days was affecting her coordination. I gently tugged her pant leg until her foot slid down to the mat, and she sat on the cushion. As I made my way around the car, I dropped the Alert Force equipment into my trunk, never to be spoken of again.

⁕

In Luke's gospel, he tells us how Jesus sent his disciples out to share the good news. In effect, he says, "Don't take any stuff with you. You don't need props or tools. You, yourself, are all the equipment you need." As I thought about these words, I talked to Jesus.

I wonder if you're asking me to do the same with Mom. Right now, I'm the one she needs, not an emergency alert button, not a home care service. Just me.

Lord, what an interesting paradox. Everything in Mom's spirit is driving her to remain independent. As I try to facilitate that by carrying out her wishes, I'm being driven to greater dependence on you. You say, "I am the vine; you are the branches. If you remain in me and I in you, you will bear much fruit; apart from me you can do nothing" (John 15:5). *It's such a contradiction. Each time I'm obedient, I expect fruit, but none appears. Ultimately, you ask me to release not only my own plans, but Mom's as well.*

This is definitely not the world's way. "Apart from me, you can do nothing." *Talk about an understatement. I don't have a hope of carrying through as Mom's caregiver unless you hold me up, equip me, and direct this crazy-making production.*

Sometimes I feel like Alice, that I too have gone through the looking glass. Still, you said I can have your peace.

Breathe,

Breathe,

Breathe,

Exhale.

Thank you for that.

Chapter Five

The phone was ringing as I walked in the door after a day at work. It was my brother.

"Hey, Lawrence. How's it going?"

"Not bad. We're getting some early spring flurries right now."

"Flurries?" I looked out the window. Sunshine and little fluffy clouds. What was he talking about?

"Where are you?"

"Home."

"At *your* home? What are you doing there?"

At Mom's request, Lawrence had arrived two days earlier. Her oven was no longer working and she needed a new one. Lawrence had been commissioned to take her to the only appliance centres Mom trusted, The Bay and Sears.

"Did you get the oven already?"

"There will be no oven. And once again I was kicked out by Mother. I came home."

I thought of his five-hour drive, and wondered how long Lawrence's old car was going to manage all this travel.

"So, what happened?" I plopped down on the couch, tucking one foot under me. Might as well get comfortable. This was going to take some explaining. "All she needed was a new oven. How could something so straightforward go sideways?"

"We went shopping," Lawrence reported, "and we looked at several ovens. She found one at Sears and it seemed to me she'd decided on it. I called over the salesman and suddenly she went ballistic. Accused me of pressuring her. I told the salesman we were apparently still thinking about it. She didn't say a word until we got in the car. "Then she let me have it. 'Why are you pressuring me? Why is it so important to you that I get an oven? Who else knows about this? I'll get an oven when I'm good and ready and I don't need your help.'

"I took her home. I tried to change the subject, asked if she wanted some lunch, but she wouldn't let it go. After an hour or so I decided enough was enough. I went downstairs, got my bag and said goodbye."

"But she was determined she needed an oven," I said, shaking my head. "She's been talking about your coming for two weeks now, bemoaning the fact that she can't bake anything."

"I know."

"Did she say anything when you left? Did she say why? Was she apologetic at all?"

"Nope. Said things like, 'Isn't it just like you to go running off when you get caught.' I asked her what I'd been caught doing and she said, 'You know. You know what you're doing.' So I politely made my exit and now I'm home."

"Oh Lawrence, I'm sorry you had to come all the way here for this. It's not right."

"Well, it's not anyone's fault. I guess we can only do what we can do. I'll call her in a few days and she'll have forgotten it all. Or act like it never happened. I can never tell which it is."

We said goodbye and I wished him well.

Now what, Lord? Do I call her right away? Wait a few days? I'd like to forget it too, but I'm remembering the last time she sent Lawrence packing.

I recalled the terrible state she'd been in, believing a man was hiding in her basement, hiding and losing her keys and wallet. I didn't want either of us to go through that again.

The next day, it felt right to call, but there was no answer.

Lord? What do you suggest? Wait another day? Hmm . . . . Peace. Okay. I'll wait. Thank you for the confirmation.

I called again the following day and this time she answered. There was no mention of Lawrence's visit.

"Hi Mom, how are you doing?"

"Well, I'm doing. But that's about it."

"I thought I'd drop by after work today for a visit. Are you free?"

"Am I free? There's nothing free, that's for sure."

I rolled my eyeballs heavenward, asking for the right words. None came. I waited silently.

"Well. I guess so. I need groceries anyway. Today? What time. Oh, honestly. Wait. I need a pencil. If I don't write it down . . . wait. What time?"

"I'll be there about three."

"Three o'clock. And we'll get groceries."

"Sure, we can get groceries. I need a few things too."

"Three o'clock. If you must," she said with a harrumph.

"I'll see you then. Bye-bye."

When I arrived, Mom opened the door to my knock. Her dark mood was in full command. The grocery trip idea had fallen by the wayside.

"What are you doing here? Why do you come here?" she demanded as I slipped my shoes off. I kept my jacket on, not sure how long I'd be staying, and followed her into the kitchen.

"You and your brother are trying to run my life. Who do you two think you are anyway?"

Her words surged and sputtered. I sat at the table and listened. There was no chance to interject as she spewed the venom she'd been nurturing. She vented. I prayed.

Lord, what do you want me to do? Am I supposed to sit and listen to her berate me when I have no idea what she's upset about? You know Mom's heart. Can you help her calm down, or at least help her tell me what's really going on?

After a time I realized there were tears mingled with Mom's fury. She grabbed a small pile of solicitation mail from the chair beside her and scattered it across the table.

"How can I keep up with this? They all write to me, all the time. How do they know who I am?"

Mom had regularly sent small donations to charities and political groups. I didn't try to explain that she was now just an address on multiple mailing lists. In her day, letters were personally written to individuals. It made sense that she believed these requests were from groups who knew her and needed her support.

"Can't you phone them?" she sputtered. "Tell them I don't want to anymore."

"You'd like to stop getting all these requests," I stated. "Shall I take them with me and deal with them?"

"Can you do that? I don't want anymore. How do I know? Will they? How many times?"

Gradually Mom's confusion calmed and she began to grasp what I was saying.

"It's hard for you to keep up with all the mail, Mom. How about I take them with me and I can mark 'Return to Sender' on the envelopes. Maybe that will stop them from coming."

"Can you do that?"

"Yes, I can." I gathered the mail and tucked it in my purse. Out of sight, out of mind.

By now it was apparent I was staying, so I slipped off my coat and hung it on the back of the chair. I plugged in her electric kettle and Mom removed a jar of canned milk from the fridge. She still considered decanting tinned milk into jars as the safest storage method.

Mom removed four chocolate biscuits from a Queen Elizabeth commemorative tin and plunked them on a plate. I dropped tea bags into stained green mugs, circa 1950, and added the boiling water. We waited for our tea to steep. As the situation calmed on the outside, I took stock of the inside.

Lord, I feel beaten up. I don't want to be here getting yelled at. I want to be in my quiet little house. How do I find your peace in this place where Mom thinks I'm the enemy half the time? I'm here because your word tells

*me to serve, but I can't hide from you the fact that I'm discouraged. I have
no idea what to do. Do you?*

A small smile curled the corners of my mouth.

*Of course you do. Then I shall wait. Take it away, Lord. You're in
charge. You run the show and I'll be the spectator. There. We have a plan.*

I removed the teabags and brought the mugs to the table. I didn't
bother making conversation. We sat in silence and sipped our tea. I
dipped my biscuit. Mom dipped hers. I couldn't think of anything
to pray, so I silently hummed *How Great Thou Art* to pass the time.
Mom pushed her mug back and forth on the table, wrinkling and
smoothing a worn linen placemat I remembered from my childhood.

Mom picked up another biscuit, scraped at the chocolate coating
with her fingernail, then put it back. We sipped our tea. I waited.

"I haven't baked cookies for ages," she said petulantly.

I thought about reminding her that that was because her oven
was broken, but my mouth stayed quiet. I nodded. I waited.

"I was baking. Cookies. I put them in the oven." A long pause.
I waited. "I forgot." Her head sagged and she stared into her mug. "I
forgot until I saw smoke coming from the oven."

With a deep, shuddering breath, she lifted her gaze, staring at me
as though she were confessing a terrible sin. Her wrinkled lids opened
wide and I saw fear in her eyes. Her shoulders slumped and her head
dropped again.

Gently, pieces slipped into place as the Lord gave me understanding.

How could Mom tell her son she didn't trust herself to bake anymore? Perhaps when she told Lawrence her oven was broken, she'd
forgotten the burned cookies. Perhaps she'd suddenly remembered
the smoke when Lawrence called the salesman over. How could she
save face? Get angry! Conjure up some irrational guilt and dump it on
Lawrence so she could maintain her dignity.

"I could have burned the house down." She stared at the useless
appliance.

"But you didn't, Mom. And you didn't replace it, so you don't have to worry it'll happen again. That was smart. We can always buy cookies, can't we?"

Mom nodded. She rose and crossed to the counter. She poured lukewarm water from the kettle into her mug and added the used teabag. She joined me back at the table, leaving the mug by the sink.

"You're always here," she said in a puzzled tone. "You're so patient. I get mad and yell at you and you're still here."

"You're going through a rough time, Mom. It makes sense that you'd be upset sometimes."

"You keep coming back. We have to get mad. We have to let each other get mad."

"And we have to keep coming back. Right? I love you Mom. I won't stop coming."

Mom reached out to touch my arm. I felt my heart melt as Jesus filled the room. I placed my hand on hers and we sat quietly for a few moments.

Jesus, I can't remember any time in my relationship with Mom when she actually reached out to me with affection. You truly do perform miracles.

❧

Driving home a little later, verses and stories from scripture began to flood my mind.

"Therefore, as God's chosen people, holy and dearly loved, clothe yourselves with compassion, kindness, humility, gentleness and patience" (Colossians 3:12).

Those are good things to wrap myself up in, Lord. I don't see any mention of clothing myself with guilt, though. I think you're telling me that Lawrence and I are to refuse any guilt Mom may try to place on us in order to protect her dignity. I'll be sure to tell Lawrence on your behalf.

I let that conviction settle in my heart as I drove the familiar streets. The low-fuel light had been on since yesterday. I pulled into a

Shell Station and parked my little Kia beside the pump. As I gassed up, another understanding flowed into my mind, one that filled me with a sense of release: *I am no longer in need of a mother.* I pondered this as I filled the tank.

The season for building a mother-daughter relationship had passed. Mom couldn't meet my emotional needs when I was young; it would be foolish to hope she could do that now. Gently this new truth flowed into my heart, and with it a realization: if I placed no expectations on Mom, she couldn't let me down.

I worked it through a little further as I paid for my gas. *Let me get this straight, Lord. You're sufficient. You cover all my needs, and that means I can meet Mom's, according to your command:* "Love each other as I have loved you" (John 15:12).

When it comes to salvation, I don't know the state of Mom's heart, but that's not my business. I need to see her as one who either is saved or who will be saved. Loving her as your child means no strings will be attached.

It's a grand aspiration, Lord, and I get it. But I don't know if I'm able to carry it out. There's so much baggage in our relationship.

Okay. So be it. I trust you to help me leave the historical mess behind so I can get on with the business of today.

Back home, I took advantage of the sunny afternoon, and hooked my dog Maggie's leash to her collar. As we walked down the snow-packed street, another verse came to mind. I couldn't help smiling.

"Go in the strength you have and save Israel out of Midian's hand. Am I not sending you?" (Judges 6:14)

Lord, that was your response to Gideon when he was arguing with you, telling you he wasn't the best man for the job. You and I both know I'm a Gideon at heart. I don't feel capable of meeting Mom's needs, and honestly, I'd rather you found someone else to do it. Forgive my lack of faith, but I may as well admit it since you know my heart already. Like Gideon, I want assurance that you're going to be with me. He asked for a sign in the form of a fleece and you met his request.

Now that I think of it, I've laid out a fleece too, over and over. When I look back at these past few weeks with Mom, I see the signs I've requested—*understanding, patience, wisdom, discernment. Regardless of my reluctance, you've equipped me moment to moment. Thank you for caring.*

Practising Lessons Learned

The air was crackling with ice crystals, the dark sky brittle with cold. I looked out the window at the bitter evening, phone to my ear, as I waited for Lawrence to pick up.

"Good evening, my sister."

I smiled, picturing Lawrence in his wood-heated northern homestead, bundled in his favourite flannel shirt-of-many-patches, imparting a formal greeting on a call-display cell phone. The man is a picture of incongruity.

"How are you faring?" he asked.

"I'm fine. I thought I'd call and give you a quick update."

"Always good—from a distance."

"Funny man! Mom finally answered her phone yesterday. I went for tea today."

"Did she mention the oven?"

"Not at first. We talked about all the junk mail she gets and she let me take it away. I'll see if I can get her off some of the mailing lists."

"Good luck with that."

"'We can but try,' as you always say."

"Very true. So she did talk about the oven eventually?"

"Yes, she did." I described Mom's story of how she'd forgotten she was baking cookies until she saw smoke rising from the oven, and her fear that she would burn the house down if she baked again. "My guess is that she didn't know how to tell you she'd done something so foolish. She didn't want you to think she was incompetent, so she yelled at you instead."

"You could be right. Or she just wanted to yell. Either way, we won't be repeating the exercise. No oven."

"No oven," I echoed. "It's like we're in an altered world when we interact with Mom. We know the language, but we don't understand the dialect. We know the person, but now she can't be who she used to be on a consistent basis, so none of us knows who we'll encounter at any given time."

"And this could be you or me one day," Lawrence said.

"Yes, it could."

I thought back to our childhood when Lawrence and I had lived under one roof. Lawrence had always gotten along well with Mom. It must be hard for him to be attacked now when he tries to help, especially since his efforts have always been appreciated in the past.

This is a different and difficult walk for all of us.

Lawrence reminded me that he didn't plan to come again for several weeks. He would wait until the risk of bad weather was past. We updated each other on our adult children and their activities and then said goodbye.

⚜

Today I was reading the story where Jesus fed the five thousand. Jesus gave thanks, and provision abounded.

Lord, I'm sorry if I don't thank you enough. I am grateful to you, every minute of every day. You've provided for us abundantly and faithfully, not just in our physical needs, but with the calm spirit you've given both Rick and me.

Today Rick came home and told me of rumours flying around work, rumours that the company is in trouble and that changes are in the offing. In the past we would have panicked, checked job listings, tightened our budget. Now the prospect of losing his job gives us a bit of a thrill, knowing that if it happens you'll take us on a new adventure, one that will be perfect for us. Today we look on such news as the possibility of an open door rather than a threat to our security. We know that whatever happens, you'll provide for both the day and the future. Most of all, we know that we're to do nothing until we have information rather than just rumours. We can wait with peace.

Learning to trust hasn't been easy. You let us go through hard times in the past so we could see you in action. Trusting you a little more each time we hit a rocky place has equipped us to have peace through the changing tides of life. Ever since the day Rick and I decided to consistently accept your place in our lives, you've faithfully sustained us.

We learned as a couple, but I had to learn individually, too. I think back to a decade ago when our daughter was injured in a car accident. She spent seven months in hospital. When Draya came home, as a family we had to learn how to manage her new life as a teenager paralyzed and in a wheelchair. I spent so much needless energy trying to plan and prepare for things I had no ability to control. When I stopped long enough to look up at you, Lord, you opened my eyes to see the helps, the supports, the solutions you were orchestrating. I kept turning back to my own strength, though, then panicking. Again you'd draw my eyes upward. Gradually, I began to register that you were managing the details all the way along. My worry and anxiety slowed us down—you moved us forward.

Today Draya's married. She and her husband run a successful home-based business. She's still paralyzed, but she lives a good, fulfilling life, and it was your doing.

Will you do the same for Mom? Mom believes in God, but I don't think she knows you, Jesus. Still, I can intercede on her behalf. I believe you hear our prayers for others, and while you won't go against their will, you do make a way when they allow it.

The world says people must take charge of their own lives. Decide what will make them successful. Find a way to get trained, maybe go into debt to do it. Equip themselves to carry out their plan, then go out to sell themselves, hoping that someone, somewhere will want their services badly enough to pay them a living wage.

The world's approach to independent living is so precarious.

Your approach is the opposite, Lord. Scripture tells us you won't re-quire anything unless you first give us what we need to accomplish it.

"*I give you God-breathed scripture. Now you are equipped.*"

"*I forgive you. Now go and forgive others.*"

"*I love you unconditionally. Now love others as I have loved you.*"

"*I fill you with the spirit of righteousness. Now you can do right.*"

The longer I walk with you, Lord, the more knowledge I gather. I'm able to take these leaps, not in blind faith, but in faith based on evidence. "Trust in the Lord" is not a Christian platitude. It's a fact I can count on, as long as I carry out my part.

I'm to obey—forgive, love, and do right.

I'm to surrender—don't force circumstances to meet my expectations.

I'm to take every thought captive—refuse the temptation to solve things that haven't happened.

Keep me on your path, Lord, and show me quickly if I deviate.

For Mom, I think her real need is to discover your love. She's always provided for herself, relied on herself, trusted no one but herself.

Does she know how much you love her? I pray you will use my hands and my lips so she can see your love through me.

"I will instruct you and teach you in the way you should go…" (Psalm 32:8).

I'll be waiting for that instruction. Thank you, Jesus.

The Flood

I was finishing lunch in the coffee room at work when the intercom began to blare. "Bobbi, line two. Bobbi, long-distance, line two."

Long distance? At work? I hurried back to my office and picked up the phone. Lawrence's name appeared on the display panel.

"Lawrence. What's up?"

"Can you call our mother? She just phoned me. It seems she's had a flood in the house."

"She called you way up north to see if you can help her here?"

"Well, at least she called! Let me know what happens."

We disconnected and I dialed Mom's number. She answered on the first ring.

"The carpet is up and down. Your brother is coming. I was sleeping. I went to the bathroom and it was wet, but I didn't want to deal with it. I went back to bed. When I got up it was still wet—all in the rooms. Not in the bedroom. It was stupid to go to sleep. I've wiped and wiped for hours and hours. I've been wiping and wringing out, and wiping and wringing out."

"I'll be there in about fifteen minutes, okay?"

"Well, I'm not sure what you can do. Your brother is coming. You should let him take care of it. Maybe it was a pipe."

"I'll come anyway. We'll see if we can figure out what happened."

"Well, all the wringing out is done. And your brother is coming. I don't know what you can do."

On the drive over I watched my brain working itself into a frenzy. How in the world would I fix this semi-defined catastrophe? *Hold it right there,* I told myself. *Lord, this is exactly what we were talking about, my tendency to run ahead of the problem and try to take control. So this is a chance to practise, right? It's a little hard to thank you for the lessons sometimes, but I certainly do thank you for the knowledge that comes with them. Two days ago, I journaled about how you go before me, how you instruct me, how you manage the details. Today it appears we're having the object lesson.*

Even if I want to take charge, I don't have enough information to make a plan. If the carpet is "up and down," that sounds like there's been a lot of water spilling onto the floor. What could have caused a main-floor flood like that? Is it still flooding? How does one remove water from a house?

As I drove, I refused to let the adrenaline rushing through my system take charge. I acknowledged the accompanying anxiety, but I tried hard to hold onto my thoughts.

Help me sort this out, Jesus.

Sort this out? Even with help I won't know what to do. I've never dealt with a flood. You're going to have to do it all. The best I can do is show up.

Suddenly I felt an unexpected calm in my spirit.

Really, Lord? Have I achieved real surrender? Okay. Go for it. I'm the assistant, you're the boss. Just tell me what to do, and I'll do it.

Humidity blasted me as I entered the house. This had been no small leak. Mom pulled me into the living room, her anxiety palpable, and my footsteps sloshed on the carpet. I left my shoes on.

"I woke up in the night," she said. "I woke up. I heard water running. I didn't want to face a problem. I wanted to sleep. I went to the bathroom but when my feet were out of my room, my feet were wet. I wanted to sleep. I went back to bed. I didn't wet the bed. The floor was wet. The hall."

She led me to the bathroom. "When I got up this morning I had to get up. That's when I came in here. See? Over the side. I stopped it now. I stopped it then. A tap was on. I left a tap on. How could I do that? I'm so stupid. Over the side. A waterfall! The floor, all to the carpets…"

I stared at the old sink, the topic of several conversations. The drain had been partially plugged for months. Rick had offered to come and snake it out, but Mom insisted only a plumber should do it. "The house is old, you know," she had said. "Anything could happen."

I had offered to call a plumber, but she had declined that as well: "I have to clean everything out from under the sink first. I can't just do that all at once!"

Considering Mom's minimalist housekeeping, 'everything' amounted to less than a dozen items, but that was beside the point. Her brain was stuck. She couldn't deal with fixing the sink herself, and she couldn't seem to accept help. For several months she'd been using the kitchen sink to wash her hands and face and brush her teeth, and was managing—until last night.

Somehow she had turned on the bathroom tap and had neglected to turn it off. Running all night long, there was nowhere for the water to go but up and over the edge.

I did a quick assessment as I looked around. "The hardwood and kitchen are pretty dry, but the carpets are soaked. How did you get so much water cleaned up all by yourself?"

"With towels." She gestured to the kitchen sink which was filled with two flowered bath towels, looking as limp and exhausted as Mom.

"I wiped and wrung and wiped and wrung and wiped and wrung. There just isn't any way. So many bits and pieces." She stood, staring at the sink, seemingly as incredulous as I was.

It was hard to imagine my tiny, ninety-year-old mother forcing her arthritic hands to wring out cold, water-soaked towels, hour after hour. The continuous bending must have been brutal. Her brain must have taken her into a mental zone of functionality as she repeated her simple but painful plan of action.

"Mom, you've done an incredible job cleaning up here." I inspected the spare room and living room. "You're right about the carpets, though. They are up and down. Heaving, I think they call it."

"Heaving. Does the basement heave?"

The basement! I hadn't even thought of that. *Mom is thinking more clearly than I am. I'm okay with that. Keep us moving, Lord. Keep us moving forward.*

"Why don't you sit for a bit, Mom. I'll go check downstairs."

The bathroom in the basement suite is located under the upstairs bathroom. Much of the water had found its way there. The old pressboard ceiling, heavy with water, had a deep sag in the middle, drips oozing steadily from the bulge.

What do I do, Lord? What do I do? I made my way back to the kitchen, reflecting again that I had never experienced a house flood before. My problem-solving skills were clearly lacking.

Not Mom's, though. As I entered the kitchen, she pointed to the bench. On it was an old copy of the Yellow Pages.

Mom's brain might struggle in the present, but it could still find experiences and strategies from the past. The phonebook was open to the plumbing section, announcing a host of problem solvers.

"I found the names." She gestured weakly to the ochre-coloured pages. "I didn't call," she said, all but whimpering.

"It would have been hard to call a plumber and explain everything," I commiserated. "But calling Lawrence was the right move. Good for you." Mom looked doubtfully at me. In her day, a man would be the one to fix such a problem, even if he were five hours away. Instead she got me.

Me and you, Jesus—and how you've come through!

"Your brother will. Where is he?"

"He's at home, Mom, on the homestead. That's why he called me. You've got everything ready, though. All I have to do is call the people who can come and help. Shall I do that now?"

"You need a plumber. I think a pipe burst."

"Or maybe it's because the sink was plugged, so it overflowed."

"Oh. Like a waterfall. I got up and it was wet. I didn't want to deal with it. I should have. I didn't. Back to bed."

"You were tired. I'm going to call a plumber now, though. I'll get someone to come and unplug that sink."

Too exhausted to raise her objections, Mom sat on the couch and watched me, her blue-veined hands worrying an old handkerchief. She had set the plan in motion; I would carry it out. I couldn't help but see this was exactly the arrangement I'd made with Jesus less than an hour before. *I'll show up. You tell me what to do.*

The first plumbing company I called wasn't available. "We don't have anyone who can come today," the receptionist told me. "But I can give you the name of a carpet cleaner who will come and suck up the water."

Suck up the water? I had no idea carpet cleaners would do that! Thank you, Jesus. My first phone call and you've solved problem number one.

I took down the name and number.

The second plumber I called was already on the road, just fifteen minutes away. He said he could swing by to assess the situation. I then called the carpet cleaning company who said a man could come within the hour.

This is going swimmingly, Lord! (Pardon the pun!)

"We're doing well, Mom. The plumber will be here soon. Then a man will come who can suck the water out of the carpets."

"Where is my wallet? I lost my wallet. Days ago. I looked and looked. And my glasses. And cheques. Where is my wallet?" Again I was amazed that Mom's thinking was so coherent. Her words were scattered, but the logic was clear. Service people would need to be paid.

"I have my credit card, Mom. I can pay for it and then you can pay me back."

"Well, I can't have you paying my bills." Mom said in a huffy tone. She got up and headed to the spare room where her filing boxes were kept. "I need to pay for it. If I can find my cheque book…" I remained in the living room.

I know it's important for her to feel independent, Lord, but I'm some-
what overwhelmed myself. I won't argue with her, but I won't help look for
the cheque book either. I'll pay by credit card. Simple as that. I might pay
again when she rebukes me for overstepping my bounds, but I'll accept that
blame in advance as long as we can keep moving forward.

I could hear her moving boxes about as my eyes settled on the kettle.

"Mom, do you want a cup of tea?" I called when the kettle began to whistle. I suspected she hadn't taken a break since discovering the flood hours earlier, and I was sure she hadn't had anything to eat or drink.

Mom came out of the spare room, an old apron in her hands and a quizzical look on her face. "There was something. Did you find it?" Her expression lightened. "Tea?"

Mom sat. I poured. I sat too. Mom guzzled the hot drink fortified with a healthy dollop of canned milk, and I poured a second mug for her. We munched some chocolate-filled cookies and silently awaited our rescuers.

The plumber arrived as promised. I smiled to myself, watching as he bent to check under the sink. The man's belt and backside perfectly corresponded to the image so often depicted in cartoons. A plunger was quickly applied to the drain, followed by a swish with the router. Soon he was on his way after charging seventy-five dollars to my credit card.

Mom didn't seem aware that a financial transaction had taken place. I was happy to leave it at that.

Somewhat revived by the tea and cookies, Mom and I relocated as much as we could off the carpets, piling boxes, books, knick-knacks and other items on the table and couch.

"Mom, take a look at this," I called to her from the living room. She peered around the corner with a stack of old magazines in hand.

"My wallet! You found my wallet!"

We carried more items to the couch.

"Mom, are these your glasses?"

"My blue ones. My good ones! And here. I have this now!" In glee she held up a pair of small silver keys, the ones needed to open the lock box where all her cash was stored. "I lost these days ago," she said in wonder.

"That's a God-wink," I told both Mom and myself. "Only he would use a disaster to solve a problem!"

The carpet cleaner arrived, dragging in a long hose attached to a tank on his van. An hour of suctioning and we no longer heard the sloppy squish of footsteps when we walked on the carpets.

"Can you take a look downstairs as well?" I asked. "The area rug down there got wet. Are you able to take it with you?"

He was, and he did. As he rolled up the sodden mat, he eyed the ceiling, still heavy and sagging under its weight of water.

"I'd poke a hole in there," he said as he walked past. "Release that water before the whole thing comes down."

Another God-wink — necessary information that wouldn't have occurred to me had the man not offered it.

Three hundred dollars was charged to my credit card, and the man left, hauling with him the hose and Mom's drenched rug. Mom sat quietly at the kitchen table, caressing her empty mug. It didn't appear she was registering the activity any longer. *That's a good thing, Lord. Let her rest and I'll do whatever else you show me.*

I scurried back downstairs, found a bucket and placed it under the lowest point of the sagging ceiling. For want of a better tool, I used a pencil to poke a hole in the soft pressboard. Water gushed out of the small hole with such force I wondered whether the ceiling would remain intact. The bucket was half-full in a matter of minutes. I dumped the bucket and replaced it to catch the steady drips. It looked as though they'd continue for a while. Now I noticed how wet all the surfaces in the bathroom were. *It must have been like a rainstorm down here!* Wet towels filled the small linen cupboard. I hauled most to the washing machine, and then I wiped and wrung, wiped and wrung, just as Mom had done upstairs.

Another job completed, I joined Mom in the kitchen, aware that I was feeling pretty weary myself.

Anything else Lord?

Nothing came to mind. We poured another cup of tea and prepared a simple lunch of buttered toast and cheese. As I ate, I marvelled at Jesus-in-action.

"You know, Mom, as I was driving over here, I prayed for Jesus to help us—and look at all he's done! The sink is unplugged, most of the water's been removed from the carpets, even the basement…" I stopped. I hadn't told her about the sagging ceiling, and I didn't feel that information needed to be shared now that the problem was taking care of itself, drip by drip. "Even the basement rug has been taken away to be cleaned."

I don't know whether Mom's taking in any of what I'm saying, Lord, but I am. I'll be telling Lawrence as well, whether he believes it was you or not.

We left the bedroom contents where we'd moved them. I told Mom I'd be back in a couple of days and we could return everything to its rightful place once the carpet was thoroughly dry.

"You must be exhausted after such a day," I commiserated as I gathered my things to leave.

"I just don't know. Anyway, here too. I just don't. So much water. Will the carpet go flat?"

"I don't know. I guess we'll have to wait for it to dry and see."

"It's old. I should replace it anyway. The roof needs to be done. The shingles are curling. Come outside. I'll show you."

"Lots of time to think about that," I said, quickly deflecting this new train of thought. "Do you have something for your dinner?"

"Soup. I have soup. The burners still work." She cast a dejected look at the oven, the cause of such distress just a week earlier. "And toast and cheese. Do you want some dinner?" Mom got up and started bustling, her brain taking her on a new track.

"Not for me, Mom. I have to get home and let the dog out. Is there anything else you need before I go?"

"I need some groceries." She glanced at the table, piled high with bedroom clutter. "I should have a list…" Mom was exhausted, her brain flipping from one topic to another.

"How about we get groceries in a couple of days, then," I recommended, making my way to the door. "I'm pretty tired now." I gave her a hug.

She pushed her slippered toe against a large wrinkle on the brightly flowered wall-to-wall carpet.

"Thank you for coming, for helping," she said with wonder in her voice, as though having someone to help with an emergency was a novelty.

"You're very welcome." I made my way out the door. "You did well, Mom. Now I know what to do if my house ever floods. This was a great learning experience!"

Mom stood at the open door until I had manoeuvred my way across the icy boulevard, climbed into my little car and pulled away from the curb. She waved. I waved, and heaved a sigh of relief.

❧

Lord, you manage things in such an amazing way when I surrender and turn them over to you. Why don't I always give you free rein? Why do I still try to be the first line of defence?

I guess it's because I feel irresponsible if I don't try to manage on my own. Everything about this world is geared towards self-sufficiency, self-reliance, self-care, and independence, but you teach a very different lesson.

"Come to me, all you who are weary and burdened, and I will give you rest" (Matthew 11:28).

"The Lord himself goes before you and will be with you; he will never leave you nor forsake you. Do not be afraid; do not be discouraged" (Deuteronomy 31:8).

You offer loving commands with promises of peace and rest attached, and yet we remain hesitant to take your words at face value.

I'm quick to get annoyed with Mom when she stubbornly tries to manage her own affairs but no longer has the capacity to do so. Do you shake your head at me, Lord, when I try to manage things I don't have the capacity to handle?

We do get it right sometimes, though. Last week Rick and I were tempted to be anxious when those rumours began about layoffs at his company. Today we learned the truth. A few years ago Rick's shop linked with a bigger corporation. Several coworkers jumped at the opportunity to move with the hope of making a little more money. Rick and I prayed for direction, but he felt no desire to make a change. Both of us wondered if it was your leading, or that Rick was simply settled in his comfort zone. Not entirely sure he was making the right decision, Rick stayed put.

Today Rick's manager called a meeting. Apparently the sister company has had a downturn and is laying people off. The manager assured his employees that they are busy and stable. Jobs are secure. Thank you, Lord!

Tuning in and listening to you...I'm getting there, Jesus, but I know I've a long way to go. Show me when I'm worrying and carrying burdens that should rightly be on your shoulders. I do it so automatically I don't even notice much of the time. Open my eyes so I can accept all that you offer.

A Second Bathroom

"I have my grocery list in my purse," Mom announced. "But first, come and look at the carpet."

As promised, I was at Mom's house, ready for a grocery trip.

Together we inspected the carpet, which had remained "up and down." The humidity, while still noticeable, was much improved. Mom had taken some of the spare-room clutter back to its home, and together we moved the rest where it belonged.

"Shall we get a treat when we get groceries?" I asked as we headed out to the car.

"Bonnie Doon," Mom responded. "There are buildings."

I understood she was suggesting we go to the Safeway at Bonnie Doon Mall, but buildings? I searched my brain for a related topic, but so far there wasn't enough information.

A few blocks down the road, Mom's plan became more clear as we crawled forward in rush-hour traffic.

"Keeping it fixed." Her sigh held a note of helplessness and she gazed at the apartment buildings stretched along Whyte Avenue. "And now the flood. How could I do that? What will I do next? I can't believe I could be so stupid. I can't keep living there."

A light dawned. "Are you thinking maybe it's time to look for a place to live that isn't so much work?

"Well, this is no good. No good. Can we drive by some places? We don't have to go in. I don't want to go in. Not to talk to anyone.

Just drive by. There are some by the mall. Places. I could walk across the street. Eat."

"If you lived near the mall you'd have easy access to restaurants and other stores for anything you'd need. Is that what you're thinking?"

"Of course."

"Living in an apartment still has challenges, Mom. You have to manage paying the bills. You have to go down to another floor to do your laundry. You have neighbours in the same hallway, and you have no choice about who they are. If they're arguing next door, you have to put up with it. And come winter, walking to the mall could be very difficult. You'd still have to cook and feed yourself."

"I suppose you're right. But where can I go?"

A clear, fully formed thought suddenly filled my mind.

Lord, Rick and I have talked about this from time to time. Should I make the offer? It feels right. Okay. Your words, please.

"Rick and I do have the basement, you know. If we were to put a bathroom in there, you'd have a pretty nice little suite to live in."

"Really?" Mom sounded shocked. "You'd let me live with you?"

"Sure we would," I told her. "We have to drive near our house to get to Safeway. Let's stop and you can take a look."

Rick was locking up the garage when we arrived. He turned to find me helping Mom through the gate.

"Rick, Mom and I were talking about the possibility of her moving into the basement," I said as he joined us on the sidewalk.

Mom looked at him anxiously.

Rick grinned and nodded. "We'd love to have you move in, Nancy." You have to love a man who can shift gears without warning.

"You could stand me living here?" Mom sounded incredulous.

"I'd love to have you live here. We'd fix it up just for you."

Overwhelmed by the offer and his expression of welcome, Mom reached up to give him a hug. Rick bent to receive it, wrapping his arms around her thin, twisted frame. "Let me give you the tour," he said as he opened the back door and ushered her in.

Rick showed Mom the finished basement, pointing out the bedroom, the sitting area, and laundry room. As I watched them, I reflected on how differently Mom responds to men as opposed to women. Maybe it's a throwback from her era when well-defined roles dictated that women were dependent and men took care of them. Mom adopts a helpless-female attitude when she interacts with men. With women, she presents a businesslike capability, intelligence and self-sufficiency. At the same time, she readily vocalizes strong annoyance when she sees other women taking on a weak, helpless role with the male gender. Driving to the house, Mom had been thoughtful and mature as we discussed the possibility of moving in. Now, with Rick, she acted like a flirtatious teen.

"Did you make this lovely place all by yourself?" she asked, looking up at him adoringly.

"Well, most of it was here when we moved in. Bobbi did the decorating."

"But I'm sure you showed her how." Mom fawned over him.

I watched their conversational dance, amused. Mom did appear agreeable to the plan, so I interjected, "If you move in, we'd want you to have your own bathroom and shower. Shall we look into putting in a bathroom?"

While Mom didn't actually verbalize assent, her words and actions were positive. Living with us felt easier than trying to acclimatize Mom to apartment living. I silently prayed, *Lord, if this is the direction to go, please open the door so we know for sure.*

Mom gave Rick another exuberant hug as he bid us goodbye. Mom was genuinely touched that he was willing to take her in. We carried on with our shopping trip. I mentioned the basement suite a few more times, but Mom didn't really engage in the conversation.

"It will take a few months to get the bathroom installed," I explained as we drove back to her house, hoping she'd be able to grasp the timeline. "It's March now. We probably wouldn't be ready for you to move until closer to summer. There's no kitchen downstairs, but you would have full use of the upstairs kitchen, and the rest of the house. Maggie would love to have you living with us, too."

"Maggie. That's your dog."

"Yes."

"Did you get the cinnamon bun? We can eat that now."

I deposited bags of groceries in her front porch. "I can take them to the kitchen for you," I offered.

"No. I have to keep doing things myself. I count them. I do inventory."

I thought about the dates I see on almost everything Mom buys, including month and year written on the tags in her clothes. I marvelled that one pair of pants was purchased in 1986.

I acquiesced and left the groceries where they sat. We shared the oversized sticky treat. Mom pronounced on various political headlines she'd been reading in *Maclean's* magazine and I listened and nodded.

Sweet tooth satisfied, we put the dishes in the sink. I offered to help wash up, but Mom insisted she would do them later. "You keep wanting to take things away. I need to keep doing things or I'll forget how."

"You make a good point," I agreed. I gave her a hug. "You keep thinking about moving into our basement, and we'll talk more about it next time I see you. Okay?"

Mom hugged me back. Her only comment was to drive safely.

Alone in the car, my mind was free to explore this unexpected development.

Can I live with my mother in the same house, Lord? With Your help, of course I can. If this is your will, if it comes about, then I know I'll have your grace and strength to be who Mom will need me to be for her. You'll equip me when the time is right.

But build a bathroom? How do we do that? Where will we find a contractor we can trust? Where do we find the money? I guess those details are your concern, not mine. The ball's in your court, Lord. Willing and waiting. That's my job.

⌒∞⌒

As the days passed I realized that anticipating this new plan was leaving me overwhelmed and drained. The challenge of living under the same roof with my mother was overshadowed by a greater anxiety, that of hiring a contractor to successfully build a bathroom. I didn't know why but it appeared that I had a strong mental block when it came to moving forward with renovations.

Lord, I'm really trying to be okay about this. Trusting you to show us how to go about hiring a contractor is my part in this venture. I know that. I also know I'm not very good at accessing peace when I'm faced with something hard.

This morning, as I prayed, I was surprised to find my mind flooded with memories of music lessons I took when I was a child. I was eight years old when I fell in love with the violin. Every Tuesday I attended the Leroy School of Music. Mr. Leroy would perform the piece we were learning for our motley crew of seven- to ten-year-olds, some squirming to get out of there, some bored but obedient, and some, like me, entranced. Even as a little girl, I was moved by the heavenly sounds emanating from Mr. Leroy's instrument.

Back home I tried to mimic my teacher's performance, but the noise emitting from my half-sized violin bore no resemblance to the music I'd heard him play. The notes were the same, the desire was the same, but the skill was sorely lacking. It would take years to accomplish even a fraction of the ability my teacher commanded.

Lord, I'm coming to realize that studying and carrying out the lessons taught in scripture is much like playing the violin.

"All scripture is God-breathed, and is useful for teaching, rebuking, correcting and training in righteousness" (2 Timothy 3:16). *This passage could be misconstrued to mean that once I know and understand your word, I should be able to make it sing in my life, like my teacher did with music on his violin, but that's not so. Paul elaborates:*

Not that I have already obtained all this, or have already arrived at my goal, but I press on to take hold of that for which Christ Jesus took hold of me.

—Philippians 3:12

Even Paul admitted he wasn't at the same level as the teacher. Lord, I'm willing to practise, just as I practised my violin as a child. I improved then. I know I'm improving now. The lessons get harder, though. The notes are more complicated. The skill required challenges me in ways I haven't been challenged before. Funny to think that building a bathroom would be a lesson in trusting God's provision, but you use everything to teach, don't you?

You and I both know, Lord, that this renovation project fills my heart with trepidation. If adding a second bathroom in our house is your plan, then I'm…well, not actively embracing the plan, but at least willing to place it in your hands, and I'm open to seeing how you put it all together. That, at least, is a statement of truth.

Thank you that your Spirit is here to encourage me, to strengthen me. Onward and..downward. (It is a basement bathroom, after all.)

God Provides

ord, my brain needs a vacation. Everything keeps tumbling around in my head like ping-pong balls in a bingo caller's cage. I know I'm supposed to cast my cares on you, but right now they're stuck to me like glue.

In her effort to stay independent, Mom is becoming increasingly dependent on me. That takes my energy.

Never knowing when Mom's state of mind is going to flip from sweet to volatile means I'm always on guard. That takes energy, too.

And now we're considering a bathroom reno. I'm trusting you to lead the way, but it seems trust takes energy as well. I keep going back to 2 Corinthians 10:5 where it says to take every thought captive. I try, but it's like herding cats. I grab one wayward thought and give it to you, and another worry breaks loose, running off on its own little tangent.

Lord, I need a distraction!

Our church had been praying for Missions Fest for the past month. I hadn't planned on going, but the flyer on my counter drew me in. I needed to be fed spiritually. The idea of spending a day in the company of hundreds of believers sounded wonderful.

Friday evening found me strolling among the booths at Shaw Conference Centre, chatting with presenters and learning about mission activities around the world. Now I sat at a banquet table, appetite satisfied, listening to the speaker. As an introvert, I felt blissfully anonymous and safe in a room full of fellow Christians.

My eyes surveyed the crowd and my thoughts drifted as I considered each person's uniqueness, each with a different story, each with passions and struggles, each known and loved by the Lord. I felt a sense of connectivity, knowing we shared a common, powerful bond in Christ. My attention was suddenly focused as I caught sight of a familiar, grey-haired gentleman. Could it be? It was! Alvin and his wife, Etta sat just a few tables away. My mind was flooded with emotion, remembering the intense relationship Alvin and I had shared a decade earlier because of my daughter.

Following the accident that left her paralyzed from the chest down, Draya spent three months at the University Hospital, followed by another four at a rehabilitation facility where she learned the basics of life in a wheelchair. Unbeknownst to us, Draya was nearing the end of her stay at the Glenrose. One afternoon the charge nurse announced that Draya was to be discharged in just ten days. "We like to get the kids home for Christmas. The doctor has okayed it. Is your house wheelchair accessible? Are you ready to accommodate your quadriplegic daughter? If not, the social worker has arranged a medical foster home. It's about two hours from here, but she says they're very good."

I remember my response. *What? God, where are you?* Tears had spilled from my eyes as I backed away from the nursing station. I stumbled down the hall to Draya's hospital room. *No one warned us this was coming so fast. What will we do? There's no money. No contractor. Winter is setting in. Ten days? Lord, help!*

With a deep breath I composed myself. I made no comment to Draya about the impending doom. After settling her for the evening, I drove the forty-five minutes to our home, sobbing, overwhelmed by helplessness. I kicked off my boots and hung my coat on the hook. The message light blinked on the answering machine. Mechanically, I picked up a pen, adjusted a notepad, and hit Play. *One more demand. One more task I'm not capable of. Lord, I don't think I can…*

"Bobbi, this is Eileen. I don't know if you remember a few months ago when I mentioned that my husband's uncle, Alvin, is a retired contractor. He's still willing to help you with renovations for Draya when you're ready. I just thought I'd remind you. Have a great day."

Now, as I looked across the conference room at Alvin and his wife, I realized God was telling me something. A verse filled my heart: "You hem me in behind and before, and you lay your hand upon me" (Psalm 139:5). *You went before us then, Lord. You had Alvin ready and waiting to meet our need and you brought him to our attention at exactly the right moment. Are you telling me you'll do the same now?*

The speaker concluded and conversation began to buzz. Quickly, I wound my way among the tables. Well into retirement when he had helped us ten years earlier, Alvin was now a frail shadow of the man I'd known him to be. His eyes were dull and his head hung low.

"Alvin? Alvin! How are you?"

Slowly his head lifted. It took a moment for recognition.

"The handicap girl," he said slowly. "We built her a room."

"We did," I nodded. "Well, you did!"

I pulled photos from my wallet, taken at Draya's wedding, and proudly shared them with Alvin and Etta.

"You made a difference, Alvin. We couldn't have done the job without you."

Etta beamed. Alvin nodded. I saw a bit of the spark from those days when Alvin had patiently tolerated my tears and helped me through weeks of chaos. After cutting a new door into our house and attaching a ramp so Draya could come home just before Christmas, Alvin settled in for the next four months, helping us build an addition onto the house. Gently he had elicited the necessary decisions from my overloaded mind. Despite my distress, he steadfastly did his job until the project was brought to conclusion and Draya had an accessible bathroom, bedroom and office space all to herself.

Lord, thank you for letting me tell Alvin how instrumental he was in helping Draya move toward independence, and for reminding me how you brought us the solution at just the right time. Of course you'll have a solution now. I just need to be patient.

I wandered past the entrance to the main concourse, still thinking about that renovation years ago. I was deep in thought when I felt a hand on my shoulder. Donna, our pastor's wife, wrapped a quick hug around me.

"I thought it was you," she said. "Did you hear the speaker?"

"I did. He was great. And I ran into an old friend, Alvin. He was the man God brought us when we needed a contractor to make the house accessible for Draya."

"I heard you're considering putting in a bathroom now. Another renovation to tackle."

"Yes." I felt my stomach clench. "And it fills me with dread. I seem to have a real mind-block when it comes to tackling renos."

"Of course you do, after managing the one for Draya." Suddenly the reason for my anxiety fell into perspective. The reno during Draya's recovery had added to an already traumatic time. Contemplating a renovation today was triggering those memories.

"Do you have a contractor in mind?"

"No. Rick and I don't know anyone, and we don't know where to begin. I wish I could twitch my nose and magically conjure up the answers!" My tone was light-hearted, but I felt unshed tears rising.

"You do know Wayne's qualified to do that sort of thing, don't you?"

"Wayne? From church? But he's a rancher."

"Yes. Rancher-slash-contractor. And I'm pretty sure he could use the work right now. There won't be much to do on the farm until spring. Why don't you talk to him?"

I walked away in awe.

Lord, did you connect me with Alvin tonight to remind me of how you work? Are you saying you're going to give us a repeat performance now, placing another qualified contractor before us, through no effort of our own? It certainly seems so.

Rick and I talked that evening, and then prayed. *Lord, if Wayne is in agreement, we'll take it to mean that you're opening the door for this bathroom addition. Praise your Holy Name! Here we are moving forward without making one phone call.*

A thought struck me. Interrupting our prayer, I looked up at Rick. "What about finances?"

We frowned in unison until I suddenly laughed in delight. "Remember a couple of years ago when Mom set up that savings account in my name?"

"Yes. There's four thousand dollars sitting there, doing nothing. Didn't she tell you it was for you to use to pay her house bills if she ended up in hospital?"

"She did. This isn't exactly the same, but do you think it qualifies?"

"Putting in the bathroom would help meet her needs, and that's what she had in mind," he mused. "Once she moves, her house can be sold and then there'd be plenty of money to cover her living expenses."

"Good point."

Lord, we're embarking on what we believe is best for Mom, and she seems to be in agreement. We're going to use her money to do it. If this is right, please keep opening doors. If not, shut it down. We're good either way. We trust you, Jesus. Amen.

The following Sunday Wayne was on greeter duty in the foyer of our small church. I quickly outlined the plan and then held my breath.

"I can't come to scope it out until Tuesday. And we'll need a permit before we start work."

"Really? You're saying yes?"

"Sounds like it to me," he said, nodding.

Lord, we're on our way

*H*elp arrived carrying a notepad and measuring tape in a battered old briefcase. Coordinating our schedules had been surprisingly easy. Wayne had to come to the city for other errands. Rick hadn't left yet for his 2:00 p.m. shift at the chrome shop where he ground, stripped and re-chromed massive rods used in mining and oilfield machinery. I was on an extended lunch hour as I had a meeting at one just down the road. Now we could go over the details together. We followed Wayne around the basement pointing out our ideas. He asked questions. We tried to give reasonable answers. Anticipating the possibility that Mom's needs could increase, we brainstormed.

The bathroom should be big enough to accommodate a walker and have room for a bench if needed. Should it accommodate a wheelchair? Irrelevant—if Mom could manage the steps down to the basement, she wouldn't need a wheelchair. A heat lamp would be nice. Should we include a buzzer in case Mom had an emergency?

"No, we'll hold off on that."

I was happy to claim and maintain ignorance as Rick and Wayne talked about electrical wiring, plumbing needs, traps, vents and other mysterious items. This renovation process was notably different from the one we'd survived ten years earlier, but there was one common thread: God had taken charge then, and he was taking charge now.

Last time, even though God had been evident, I'd kept myself in a state of anxiety, never truly grasping that I could let go and leave the details to the Lord. This time, I realized, I was able to appreciate

God's presence and trust him. It felt very different and I welcomed the change.

About to leave, Wayne asked, "When do you need this done by?" Rick and I looked at each other. Rick shrugged.

"That's up to God," he said. "When you get it done will be when we need it."

A convoluted answer? Wayne didn't think so. He nodded, indicating full understanding. He closed his worn briefcase, shook hands and was gone.

Lord, working with another believer who listens to you really puts a different flavour into the mix. Thank you for connecting us with Wayne.

Wayne spent the rest of the week drawing up plans. He reviewed them with us one more time. The following week I booked a morning off work and took his simple freehand sketches downtown to apply for the building permit.

Here we go, Jesus. All week long people at work have been telling me horror stories about the city planner's office. Allen lost two days of work trying to get his permit. Jen got a fifty dollar parking ticket because it took so long. Nora's husband had to return over and over when the city requested additional information. Because Rick and I are the homeowners and Wayne isn't a professional contractor, we are, in effect, doing this reno ourselves. I have to apply for it and answer any questions they might have. Wayne's explained details about items they might question. You know I don't really understand them, though.

Okay, Lord. You and I seem to have come to this understanding over the past few months, so I'm going to follow the same plan. I show up, and you talk me through it. I'm fine with coming back a few times if that's what it takes. I'm trusting you to give me the words to say, and to understand whatever objections they come up with so I can pass those on to Wayne.

Oh, and a parking space would be nice. Thank you, Jesus!

Unfamiliar with downtown parking, I was excited to find a convenient lot on the same block as my destination. Optimistically, I paid for just two hours and stuck the ticket on my dash. Wayne's plans were tucked in a bright yellow folder. I scanned them one more time.

Lord, can I place one more fleece before you? I want you to know that I'm fine with shutting this whole thing down, if that's your decision. I'm assuming you want us to go ahead, given how easily this is coming together, but if barriers start to get in the way, Rick and I will take that as a "no" from you. If that's the case, I know you'll have something else planned for Mom. So here's my fleece. Today is a perfect moment for you to put a stop to this. I'll assume the door is open unless you slam it shut. Please don't let it swing back and forth, though. I'm easily confused.

I'd never been to the city planning department before. Their well-posted instructions showed me how to negotiate what looked like a maze, but one that was laid out clearly, deliberately and efficiently. Signage told me where to stand, where to sit, where to take a number, where to wait in the next queue. Step by step, I moved from station to station, feeling like a widget on an assembly line. It took all my concentration to follow each arrow, find the next seating area, locate the number dispenser, and watch the right display board that would announce the next clerk's availability. I was so caught up in the process that I barely paid attention to the conversations I was having as I moved from clerk to clerk. Suddenly I realized the lady before me was pointing across the room.

"Over there. You can pay by cash or credit card."

I was puzzled.

"What am I paying for?"

"Your permit." She spoke kindly, deliberately as if she thought I was a little dense.

"You mean I passed?"

"You don't pass, Mrs. Junior. You apply and you're approved. And yes. You're approved. Over there. You can pay by cash or credit card."

She looked pointedly at the *Vacant* light that was flashing by her desk, indicating she was ready to serve the next person.

I gathered my papers in a bit of a daze.

Seriously, Lord? That's it? There were no questions. They didn't challenge anything. I have two notes to give to Wayne written by one of the inspectors, so I don't have to explain any details either. It went so smoothly, I have to believe we're on the right path. Thank you for your attention to the details. Thank you that you're going to pave the way for us to find all the right materials, and any help Wayne might need. Thank you that I won't get a parking ticket. I have fifteen minutes left! You are the Master, Lord! We're on our way!

I exited the lot and drove home with praise songs in my heart. Could it really be this easy?

The next morning a conversation with Wayne confirmed we were indeed on our way. He already had a number of the materials purchased. Work would begin the next day.

I was excited to call Mom and tell her everything was coming together. Wayne felt three months would allow enough time to complete the job, and give some leeway to allow for his ranch duties. I planned to tell Mom she could move in around June.

Our dog, Maggie, was curled beside me on the couch. I scratched her tummy as I waited for Mom to pick up.

"Good morning. How are you?"

"Where have you been?" she demanded. "They could come any day now. It's already March."

Her unexpected attack caught me off guard.

Lord, what's going on? Help me, please!

"I'm not sure who you mean, Mom."

"They're going to come for money. For the rent here. I have to stay in this room all the time."

"You're not renting there, Mom. That's your house. You own it."

"What are you talking about?" Her voice was strident.

"It's your house Mom," I said, trying to be matter-of-fact. "You bought it forty years ago. You taught school to pay off the mortgage and you own it outright."

"How do you know all this?"

I didn't know how to answer. I stayed quiet.

"What are they giving you that information for anyway? They should be giving it to me. You just have to butt into everything, don't you?"

"Mom, do you remember last week we were talking about you moving? You said you wanted to look at renting an apartment, and then we came and looked at the basement here at my house. Rick told you we'd love to have you move in and live with us. We talked about adding a bathroom."

Suddenly her tone changed abruptly. "Oh, we couldn't do that. You need your privacy."

We need our privacy? Or did she? When Lawrence is here Mom often tells him he's tired and should go lie down. He says he's figured out that she really means she's tired, but for some reason she can't own the feeling, so she projects it on him. Is that what she means now? She needs her privacy?

"People can't live on top of each other," she said forcefully. "They end up hating each other. And I could never live underground again."

Underground? Oh. The basement is underground. When I was little, we lived in the basement suite of our house for three years while Dad built the upstairs. That was a bad time in my parents' marriage. Is she saying the idea of living "underground" isn't an option now?

"You don't want to live in a basement again. Is that what you're saying?"

"Tell Rick it's nothing personal. I just can't do that."

"I'll be sure to tell him. I know he won't be upset."

"Then can he find me someplace else to live? I have to leave here in March."

"Who says you have to leave, Mom?"

"Those people. They make me stay in my room all day. All night. I can't come out. And now you say they're telling you about this house, that it's my house. It can't be mine if they're telling you about it. Who do you think you are, finding out about my personal business? Who is this telling you these things?"

Lord Jesus, help me! It seems that trying to grasp the concept of renting and moving has caused random neurons to begin firing in Mom's brain. This level of confusion has never happened before. What can I say to give her some peace?

Our conversation went back and forth with no resolution. Eventually she quit arguing with me.

"If you think you know so much about my house, then I guess I just have to believe you," she said, still frustrated, but somewhat resigned. "All this talk is foolish anyway." I quickly took the opportunity to change to a less volatile subject.

"I tell you what. The snow should be melted in another week. Why don't we go for a walk down Whyte Avenue and do some window shopping."

"The sun has to shine sometime." Mom gave a weak laugh. I recognized it as one she offers when she wants to make peace.

"Yes, the sun certainly does have to shine sometime. Give me a call if you need anything. I'll be in touch in a week or so for a grocery trip."

"I guess you will," she concluded. "Goodbye."

Rick and I sat down, the bright yellow folder between us. I filled him in on my conversation with Mom. Absently I traced the shape of the cross on the table while he digested this new twist. We held hands and wondered what to do. Finally we laid it out before the Lord as clearly as we could.

Jesus, it seems to us that you're the one who started this process of building a bathroom. It's not something we would have considered for any reason other than having Mom come to live with us. You knew that, so we have to believe you allowed those circumstances to come together to kickstart the process. The only door that seems to have closed is Mom's desire to move in. Will Mom change her mind at some point and come after all? Will the bathroom be needed for someone else?

We paused in our prayer. I waited. This was one of those times I wished God would light up a neon sign saying *Stop* or *Go*. It didn't happen. I looked into Rick's calm blue eyes. He returned my gaze.

"Let's go for it," he said. "I don't see any doors shutting. God's found a contractor. God's shown us the money. God's got us an approved permit. Seems to me like we're in his will."

"Ya think?"

"I think."

"Then fine. Decision made. We're building a bathroom."

Early Friday morning Wayne arrived and demolition began. The toilet would be situated under the stairs. The shower and sink would consume some of the oversized bedroom's space. Walls came down quickly. When I got home from work I was amazed to see a trench had already been jack-hammered through the concrete in preparation for the pipes. The job was underway!

Another Fall

Despite the difficulties Mom and I had in our relationship over the years, Mom has always thought highly of her grandchildren, and they of her. When Draya was little she informed me, "Grandma makes sure there is butter in every hole of the Eggo Waffles. You should learn from her, Mom."

Now in their mid-twenties, Draya and her brother Luke understand the tumultuous nature of my relationship with my mother. They also know it warms my heart that they get along so well with Grandma.

On this snowy Saturday, Draya and I were shopping, making our way through her list of stores, searching for a new couch and chair for their living room. As we drove from one mall to another, I told her how Uncle Lawrence and I had tried to help Grandma set up home care and then the alert button service but both had failed before they had even begun.

"That must have been so frustrating," Draya commiserated. "You try and try, and nothing works."

"Yeah, it is. It's getting harder and harder to make myself visit her, knowing she's probably going to start us off on another wild goose chase. She needs the company, but the confusion is as stressful for me as it is for her."

My neck and back are always aching these days. Stress. What a pain—literally. Consciously I'm fine with helping Mom. Subconsciously it's another story. As much as I try to relax, anxiety and stress have built to the point where I'm tying myself up in knots.

As we sat at a red light I rolled my head to the right and to the left, trying to relieve the tension.

"All knotted up, are you?" Draya knows me well. "What makes Grandma so stressful?"

"Just being alone with her, I think. Trying to decode her conversation, figuring out what she's saying, second-guessing what she might need and hoping not to guess wrong, causing her to blow up. It takes a toll."

"So why don't we have a family get-together at our house?" Draya offered. "Then we can all share the stress."

We made a plan for the coming weekend. As theirs was the only wheelchair-accessible house, Draya and her husband Matt would host the gathering. Our son Luke agreed to come and enjoy a home-cooked meal. Rick, Mom and I would round out the guest list.

That Sunday Rick dropped me off so I could help Matt set up a simple buffet; Rick carried on to pick up Mom. None of our family likes to cook formal dinners and potlucks are our mainstay. Mom insisted on bringing something, so she and Rick stopped at Safeway where she bought a bag of cookies. Luke brought pop, I contributed a Crock Pot of chicken stew, and Draya and Matt provided the salad and dessert.

Mom carried herself with dignity when Rick brought her in. She seemed very much in control, and pleased to be taking part in a family gathering. Rick hung up her coat, and everyone exchanged hugs and hellos. We sat around the living room, catching up on stories about work, pets, cars and winter.

The kids made a good effort to include Grandma in the conversation, but normalcy slipped away as it became clear Mom couldn't follow what was being said. Perhaps it was her hearing or perhaps it was the volume of information being volleyed back and forth. In any case, within a few minutes her awareness drifted away. She settled back in the big armchair and appeared content to watch everyone and simply enjoy the bustle and noise. Draya and Matt have two cats and the sociable one, Kingston, paraded majestically around the room and then presented his hairy self to Mom, leaping delicately on her lap. Mom thoroughly enjoyed his attention.

The men chatted about the merits of two opposing teams playing football on the muted TV. Once in a while Mom would make an observation, but when I caught her words, I realized she was on another topic altogether.

"The grass is always so green this time of year," she pointed out to no one in particular.

I glanced at the turf on the televised football field. Mom never watches television, but given that the ground outside was covered with snow, I decided the field was the topic of her discussion. "That grass really is green, isn't it," I said, jumping onto this semi-plausible subject. Luke glanced over and took my cue.

"Yeah, Grandma. They play football on some pretty nice grass, don't they?"

Mom smiled and nodded, and returned to her own thoughts while the conversation carried on.

Lord, I so appreciate how relaxed the young people are, how accepting of what some might see as unreasonable behaviour. I still feel I need to run interference for Mom, but it's much easier when the rest of the family shares the responsibility in carrying the conversational ball. I'm so glad Draya came up with this idea.

We indulged in our communal dinner, and then sat in the living room to enjoy pie and ice cream. Mom finished her dessert.

"I'll just take this to the sink," she said, rising. As she walked back into the living room, her stocking-clad foot slipped on the hardwood and suddenly she was down on the floor. It happened so fast that we all just stared. Rick was first to react and was at her side in a flash. My mind was trying to formulate a plan of action: don't move the person, check for broken bones. Before I could open my mouth, Rick had lifted her into the air as though she were a life-sized doll. She was so small and frail that it looked like she weighed nothing at all as Rick lifted her with strong hands and deposited her on her feet. Mom quickly made her way to her chair. She didn't appear to be hurt but she was very distressed.

"I'm fine. I'm not hurt," she said in a defensive tone. "I should have worn slippers," she berated herself. "It's such a slippery floor."

"It is Mom,"I agreed. "Very slippery. You're sure you're okay?"

"It's late. You don't need to stay here so late. You must be tired," she announced fretfully.

I took my cue that it was time to take her home, and we gathered her coat and purse. She carefully sat down to pull her boots on, then gave everyone hugs and thanked Draya for hosting the dinner.

"You're very welcome, Grandma." Draya hugged her back. "I'm glad you could come. We'll have to do this again sometime."

Rick offered to stay and help Matt clean up. Mom and I made our way carefully to the car.

Lord, I don't see any sign of pain. My goodness, she could have broken a hip. Thank you for protecting her.

Mom's agitation continued as we drove. "One fall isn't enough to mean someone needs to be put away," she muttered to the windshield. "It was just one fall. My foot slipped, you know. I should have brought slippers. The floor was slippery. People need to allow people to do that. To fall. And not overreact. Maybe another time we'll talk about it. Yes, another time."

Is Mom afraid we'll use her fall as evidence to force her out of her house? It certainly seems that way.

"You're right," I tried to reassure her. "That floor is slippery. I'm just glad you weren't hurt."

Oblivious to my assurances, she muttered on, building her argument, not letting me get a word in either for or against. I navigated the roads, and since I couldn't join in her conversation, I asked the Lord to intervene for me.

Jesus, can you give Mom peace? She's so upset. I don't want to drop her off at home thinking we're going to call someone to have her put away. I don't know how to get through to her. Can you help me?

As we turned into her neighbourhood, I had a sudden inspiration.

"It's going to be spring in another month," I remarked loudly. Since this was totally off topic, I reiterated my theme. "I can't wait for spring. It'll be great to take my little dog for long walks again. You like walking, don't you, Mom? Maybe you and I can take the dog for walks together when it's nice again."

"Walk a dog?"

"Yes, Maggie. Our little Bichon-Shih Tzu. She loves going for walks. Do you want to join us when it's nice out?"

"I walk all around the neighbourhood. Not on the ice. I wait. When it's dry."

"Yes, when it's dry we'll take Maggie for a walk."

"That would be very nice," Mom said, smiling now. She sounded satisfied, and relaxed with the idea that we had a plan down the road that couldn't happen if we put her into a home.

We arrived at her house and I helped her over the snow banks by the curb. "You go on now," she said. "I can get in by myself."

I wanted to walk her to her door, but I wasn't going to push it.

As I made my way to the driver's side, I said a little prayer. *Thank you for helping me change the subject, Lord. Please get Mom back into her house safe and sound.*

She remained on the sidewalk and waved as I pulled away from the curb.

As I drove, I pondered Mom's need for independence. In her world, independence trumped relationship. She called on me when things when awry, but sent me packing as soon as she felt she was back in control.

I can't point fingers, though. Isn't that what I do with you, Jesus? When I'm drowning I call on you for help, and there you are. You support, you provide, you teach, you untangle and you love. Then, as soon as things stabilize, it's "Thanks Lord, I'll take it from here."

Will we ever learn? It's not about the help, it's about the relationship! Don't stop teaching me, Lord. Your peace is my greatest desire. That and your wisdom in taking care of Mom. How would I ever manage this without you? Thankfully, I don't have to.

Enter the Irishman

Chapter Twelve

"Bobbi, line four. Bobbi, line four. Lawrence calling."

What? Not again! Uttering a quick apology, I ducked out of the management meeting that had just convened and hurried to my desk. Call display showed Mom's number. *Whew! Not long distance. I guess I can assume there's no crisis. Lawrence must be visiting.*

"Hey, brother. I didn't know you were coming to town. When did you get in?"

"An hour ago. Mom called me yesterday and said she needed me here for a very important meeting. I thought she'd already told you."

"Nope. This is the first I'm hearing about it. What's the topic?"

"Selling the house." He paused, waiting for the reaction he knew was coming. It took me a moment to process the information.

"Seriously?"

"Seriously. She got hold of some fella named Luke Flanagan. He's a realtor who works in the area. I take it she saw his ads. Apparently he's coming at two-thirty and you and I are expected to join them. She says she doesn't want to sell yet. Just wants to know about the process."

"Wow! A start! That's good enough for me. Two-thirty? I should be able to make it. I'll see you then."

We rang off and I scurried back to my meeting.

Sell the house, Lord? Mom's considering some serious matters. Sounds like she's going slowly, but this still has to be hard for her. Can you help us this afternoon, please? Make sure the right things are covered? Help Mom to grasp what she'll need to know and understand. I don't know this Flanagan fellow, but I pray he'll be helpful. And respectful. Never a dull moment!

Our meeting wrapped up an hour later. I had little recollection of what had been discussed. My mind was clearly elsewhere. Luckily I'd scribbled a page of notes to refer to the next day. I popped my head into our executive director's office and gave her a brief rundown.

"Go and take care of your Mama," she told me.

"Thanks, Janet. I'll make up the time tomorrow." I went back to my desk and powered down my computer.

Lord, I'm so thankful my boss understands. Her father-in-law has been living with her family for a few years now. They're having similar experiences with Grandpa. Thank you for placing me in a job where people matter more than money.

The day was cool and sunny. Most of the snow was gone now. As I drove, I considered the ramifications of this meeting, but quickly put the brakes on my train of thought.

This is yet another opportunity to practise the simple act of obedience you keep asking of me, isn't it Lord?

1. Mom calls.

2. I show up.

As a job description, it couldn't be more basic.

I'm glad I'll have Lawrence as company this time. I still have a little anxiety, but not much. I cast that on you, Jesus. Please help us accomplish whatever is right according to what you know Mom needs.

Lawrence met me at the door of Mom's house. Voices drifted from the kitchen.

"How's it going?" I asked softly as I removed my coat and boots.

"So far, so good. He's a nice guy."

We joined Mom and the realtor at the table.

Luke Flanagan was a tall Irishman with curly salt-and-pepper hair. He radiated positive energy.

I recalled Mom mentioning his name during past conversations when she'd reflected on "the need to move when the time comes." She never called him Luke, or Mr. Flanagan—always, "Flanagan."

I introduced myself and shook hands. Mom brushed aside the niceties.

"I need to know how you'll do this," she said, ignoring me and directing the conversation back to the topic at hand. "Where will I live when you sell the house?" Her tone was professional, businesslike. This was the Nancy of a decade ago. It was encouraging to see that strong, confident woman taking charge.

Flanagan responded in kind. "We won't be sellin' the house until you've found a new place to live, Nancy." His Irish brogue was appealing. "First you move out, then we put it on the market." Flanagan spoke slowly, clearly, most of all, respectfully.

"Will you find me a new place then?" she inquired.

"If you want to buy a house, then yes, I would help you do that. But if you're goin' to move to a seniors' lodge, you should set that up yourself. Your son and daughter will help you."

Lawrence and I nodded vigorously, but Mom took no notice. This was between her and Flanagan.

Apparently Flanagan didn't share Mom's view, as he addressed all three of us. "Me wife and I have just moved me mom-in-law to a lodge. They call it assisted livin'. She's been havin' some trouble rememberin' things and all, as sometimes happens, you know. The place she's in seems nice and she's gettin' used to it bit by bit."

I was flabbergasted.

Lord, not only did you direct Mom to this gentle realtor; he also has full comprehension of the situation because he's living it.

Flanagan turned back to the task at hand. In a strong, easy-to-hear voice, he explained how a house sale would work.

He's picked up on Mom's poor hearing, as well. This just keeps getting better and better!

A silver folder with royal blue lettering appeared from his briefcase. He turned all his attention to Mom, but made sure Lawrence and I had a good view. Flanagan neatly laid a series of flyers across the table in front of Mom, each depicting a property in the area. Speaking as a professional to a valued client, Flanagan described the similarities and differences between the houses on the flyers and Mom's house. He highlighted each price as he led Mom through the market comparison analysis.

Was Mom understanding? Her eyes were engaged, but for the most part, they were focused on the realtor. I had the sense she was waiting for an opening to interject, but she held her tongue until Flanagan had concluded his presentation.

"What about an apartment? Can you find me an apartment?"

Market value was not an issue. Selling didn't seem to matter, either. Moving topped Mom's list and she seemed determined to have Flanagan act on her behalf.

Lord, is it that Mom wants to manage her affairs herself? Or does she not trust Lawrence and me to act in her best interests?

I began to wonder how this meeting had come about. Thinking back, I recalled Mom's efforts to initiate contact with the home care company. I had found several script-like notes she had written. "I am calling about your ad. I'm a senior and I would like to meet." Had she written a script before calling Flanagan? Had he picked up on her confusion during their conversation? Maybe Flanagan had been the one to insist Mom have her children at this meeting. Hence, her call to Lawrence yesterday, demanding that he come immediately. It seemed a reasonable deduction, given the fact that Mom was pointedly ignoring my brother and me. No, our attendance was not her wish.

"An apartment," Mom repeated.

"I don't deal in apartments, Nancy." Flanagan was patient but steadfast. "I only deal in houses. But you'll have time to find the right place first."

"How long will it take?"

"To find a new place to live?" Flanagan included the unwelcome children once again. "I know sometimes it takes a while but we were able to find a place for me mom-in-law in just a few weeks. If you get your name on a waitin' list, there can be an openin' pretty fast."

"So when will you sell it?" Mom asked.

"Not until you have a place to live. First, you find the right place for you, Nancy. Then you call me, or get your son or daughter to call me."

"And you'll help me find a new place?"

"Only if you want to buy a house. I only help people buy and sell houses."

"I'd like an apartment. The ones by the mall. By Bonnie Doon. Do you know those ones?

"Yes, I know those ones. But I don't deal in rentin' apartments."

"Someone must. Who would do that? Do you know who?"

"That's somethin' your son and daughter can help you with. Or they can help you find a nice lodge."

"Do you have papers for the lodge?"

"No. I only deal in buyin' and sellin' houses…"

In my head I heard a melody begin..

"*This is the song that never ends…*"[1]

Lawrence, too, recognized that Mom's brain was starting to loop. After the third revolution he stood firmly and reached out his hand. "Well, thanks a lot, Luke. This has been a great help. You've given us all we need to get started. Mom can look at the information and decide what she wants to do next."

Mom gave Lawrence a furious look, as if to say, "What are you doing? I'm not done yet!"

Flanagan and I rose as one. He shook hands all around and turned his full attention back to Mom. "You have a good property here, Nancy. I don't think I'll have any problem sellin' when the time is right. You don't have to rush, though. You listen to your son and daughter. They know what's needed and they'll be a big help to you. Just like me wife and I were a help to me mom-in-law."

---

1 Writer/composer Norman Martin, 1988.

Lord, thank you for this endorsement. Maybe Mom will listen to the realtor and believe Lawrence and I can be trusted.

Flanagan handed each of us a business card. He left the flyers of local houses for sale, along with an information booklet, *When You're Ready to Sell*, for Mom. She stood up, lifted her head and squared her shoulders as she saw Flanagan to the door.

⤷✠⤶

Jesus, my Jesus. You love Mom so much! I could see how encouraged she was to be treated with respect, to have her opinion valued. She struggles day to day, but this afternoon Flanagan treated her with regard, as someone worthy of a professional business interaction. She was always so self-sufficient—capable of researching topics, making good decisions. I can't imagine the loss she must feel when her brain keeps betraying her. I know it was you who directed Mom to Flanagan. Even when she asked the same question again and again, his response was deferential. Thank you for affirming Mom that way.

Lawrence and I were greatly encouraged, too, knowing there's a realtor Mom's chosen herself, someone she trusts to sell her house when the time comes. Every aspect of this meeting was of you, Lord. I keep going back to Psalm 139. You go before and behind. You're preparing the way for all of us, aren't you?

Just one little concern, Jesus. Mom seems determined that Flanagan will help her find a new place to live. She wants his help, not mine or Lawrence's. We'll need your assistance to deal with this when the time comes.

Chapter Thirteen

*M*aggie greeted Lawrence with wild barking and excited leaps, buffeting his knees with her paws. Lawrence wrestled out of his jacket and climbed over the dog, laughing at her antics.

I hung the proffered jacket in the closet. "Good to see you. I take it your car behaved on the way here?"

"It did," he said, gathering Maggie onto his lap as he made himself comfortable on the couch.

"What's your plan?" I asked.

"Right now? A cup of coffee and a break from Mom!" He grinned ruefully.

This was Lawrence's third trip to Edmonton in two months. We'd finally seen the end of an interminable winter. The safer roads allowed an additional item on his agenda.

"Tomorrow morning I'm going to take Father with me to Calgary for a couple of days. Visit the relatives there."

"Dad will love that," I called out from the kitchen as I started a pot of coffee. "It's been years since you and he have had a few days alone together." Lawrence always made a point of having breakfast with our father and stepmother the morning he drove home from his visits to the city. This time Dad would get some coveted one-on-one time with his son.

I joined Lawrence in the living room while the pot brewed. "Are you going to stop in when you get back, or just head straight up north?"

"I think I'll stop for another night or two with Mom. We talked today about how she's doing. She was quite distraught. I get the sense that she's starting to frighten herself with the way she's behaving some of the time."

"We've been noticing things for a while. Now she's admitting it? That's quite a change. Did she give specifics?"

I brought mugs of coffee into the living room. The afternoon was dreary; the room felt dark. I switched on a lamp, but it didn't help to brighten the atmosphere.

"Counting," Lawrence nodded a few times, then took a sip from his mug. "After Flanagan left, I drove her to the bank and she took out her usual two thousand dollars for household expenses. When we got home she told me I was tired and should go and rest…"

"Oh no," I interrupted. "Did she lock you in the basement again?"

He laughed. "Not this time. She was sitting at the table, counting her cash, so I figured she wanted some privacy. I went downstairs to read for a couple of hours. Had a nap. When I came back up she was still sitting at the table. I don't think she'd moved."

"What had she done with the cash?"

"Nothing. She was still counting it. I thought maybe some was missing so I asked if it was all there. She looked at me and threw her hands up like I'd caught her doing some terrible deed. She suddenly burst out with, 'I can't quit counting it!' I guess she'd been sorting and organizing and re-counting and re-sorting over and over since I'd gone downstairs. I suggested she break it up into smaller amounts and put it into envelopes. Then it would be more manageable. Just take one at a time when she goes shopping."

"Did she like that idea?"

"I don't think it registered. She sounded totally disgusted with herself. Said she hates it when she starts this. That she watches herself sorting and counting and can't stop. Called it 'crazy behaviour.' Her words, not mine. She said sometimes she does it for hours on end. It's exhausting."

"Like obsessive-compulsive behaviour?"

"I guess so. Anyway, I piled it up and put it back into the two bank envelopes and asked where she wanted it for now, so we could make some supper. She looked really confused, so I just tucked it into her lockbox in the spare room. Do you know where the key is for that box?"

"Not any more. She keeps moving it around."

"Well, it's not in the lock. At least she can't lock the money away and misplace the keys."

"True." It seemed like strange rationale, to put cash into an unlocked lockbox for safe keeping, and be relieved the keys were missing.

Lord, the application of logic has changed since dementia came into the picture. The focus is on what works, not what makes sense. We really need your guidance to know what's right in Mom's no-longer-conventional world. Sometimes she's perfectly reasonable. Other times, her brain can't grasp the simplest of concepts. From her conversation with Lawrence, it seems she's able to step back and watch herself as this happens. It must be so disturbing. Please keep your hand on her, and on us, so we know how to support her the best way we can.

We finished our coffee. Lawrence stood and took a deep breath.

"Well, here I go," he said with mock confidence. Fortitude mustered, he gathered his coat and shoes. With each new event, both of us found re-entering Mom's world an increasing challenge.

I walked him to his car. "How long will you be gone?"

"Father and I will head out first thing in the morning. Two days should be enough. I expect to be back by Friday. I'll give you a call then."

"Sounds good. Dad's going to have a great time. It's been ages since he was on a road trip."

"I think our stepmom will enjoy having some quiet time, too."

"You're probably right." I smiled. Dad could be a handful. Almost ninety, he insisted on traveling the city by bus, and often forgot to turn on his cell phone, making it hard for our stepmom to keep tabs on him. "Drive safely!"

Lawrence nodded, and cranked the engine. He turned and gave me a wry grin, then slowly drove away. Even the car seemed reluctant to return to the potential chaos of Mom's world.

Maggie was waiting at the door, her vibrating body indicating she expected to go out as well. I gave her a scratch, and reached for her leash. Walking was always a good time for prayer, and I felt the need to process some of Mom's struggles.

Jesus, Mom's brain seems to be in worse shape these days. The long winter has taken a toll: no sunshine, no exercise, and trapped in her house with no outside stimulation. Is this recent behaviour a true reflection of Mom's present brain capacity, or is this partially environmental?

Now that the weather is improving she can get out more. Perhaps her capacity will increase again. She can go for walks in the sun, see the outside world, have other things to think about instead of staying trapped in her own small world.

If she doesn't improve, what steps can we take to help out? Not having power of attorney or any authority to make decisions on her behalf means she has full control over her affairs, whether she can manage them or not. I know the legal system is set up to prevent abuse, but at times like this it prevents help as well.

Our hands are tied. Once again, I leave it in yours.

Bless Lawrence and Dad on their trip. Give them good memories. Bring them safely home.

❦

Two days later with Rick still on the late shift, I was relaxing with a solitary dinner. Our local news anchor filled me in on the day's events while I finished my casserole. Maggie heard Lawrence's arrival before he could knock. She flew to the door, spinning in a wild dance of frenzied barking.

"Settle down," I told her, muting the TV. I opened the door to find my disheveled, red-eyed brother slouched against the frame, suitcase in hand. He dropped his head dramatically.

"Oh my!" I swung the door wide to let him enter. "Coffee?"

"Sure."

"Dinner?"

"No."

"Sit."

"Thanks."

"You're staying here tonight?"

"It would appear."

Maggie scrambled onto his lap and he slowly stroked her silky ears. I took my dinner plate to the kitchen and started a pot of decaf. Filling the sink so the dishes could soak, I set out a couple of mugs. When the pot was ready, I poured our coffee then joined Lawrence in the living room. He hadn't moved.

"Maggie's good for the soul, isn't she?" I set his cup on the end table beside him.

"At least something's good."

"Okay. Tell me the story."

"Tell you the story. Blood. Blood and Money."

"What?"

Lawrence lifted the hot mug in his hands and consciously relaxed his body. He laid his head back against the sofa and closed his eyes. "It was like a battle had taken place in the kitchen," he said, eyes still closed. "Blood everywhere! But I'm getting ahead of myself."

I waited, impatiently. *He's here. Things must be okay now. But what happened?*

"We had a good trip, Father and I. Nice visit with the relatives. Stayed at my son's. Father played with his great-granddaughters. Good trip. Yup."

"I'm glad." I wanted to shake him, but I held my peace. Lawrence sometimes entertains a touch of the dramatic—this was one of those times.

"We got in today around noon. I took Father home, then went directly to Mom's. I didn't bother knocking. She rarely hears anyway. And she knew I was coming. So I let myself in the back door.

"The kitchen was covered, I mean *covered*, in blood. Splashes. Blotches. Smears everywhere. Like someone had been stabbed or something!"

My mouth gaped. "How could there be blood everywhere? Was Mom hurt?"

He opened his eyes and shook his head in wonder. "A nosebleed. She had a nosebleed."

"A nosebleed?"

"Apparently. It started around 8:00 a.m., she said. She sat down with a tissue until it stopped. Then she got up to clean the mess. And then it started bleeding again and she'd go sit down. Then back up to clean, as soon as it stopped…"

"You got in at noon? And this started at eight? Was it still bleeding?"

"Oh yeah. You wouldn't think one little woman could produce that much blood! Wads of tissue everywhere. She was using bloody tissue to wipe up the new splotches, smearing them—on the counter, the floor, the sink, the stove, the table, the door, the walls…everywhere her hands touched, more blood was smeared." He took a few sips of coffee. "I tried to get her to sit down so it could clot. She was having none of that."

"Why didn't you call me? I could have come and helped."

"I suggested it. She blew up. 'No way,' she said. 'Your sister's too bossy. I don't want her here telling me what to do.' So I became bossy myself. I pretty much forced her to sit in the chair and stay still while I started cleaning up. Keeping her put was almost as challenging as cleaning the mess."

"Oh, Lawrence! What an afternoon you've had."

"That wasn't the end of it!"

"There's more?"

"Yes. But let me put my bag downstairs. I'll have a quick shower and change. Then I'll tell you the rest."

As I washed the dishes I thanked the Lord for the lovely bathroom Wayne had completed about a week before. We hadn't finished all the painting yet, and Rick wouldn't get to the baseboards until his next day off, but Lawrence had a functional shower and privacy as he unwound from his traumatic day. I couldn't imagine what more there could be to this disturbing narrative but dementia seems to have a way of creating some wild tales. I tidied the kitchen as I waited for Part Two.

Having put the dishes away, I scooped out two small bowls of ice cream, acting on my belief that ice cream has a medicinal, calming effect in times of crisis. I awaited Lawrence's return, and considered Mom's comment that I was too bossy.

Mom often tells Lawrence my faults, Lord. I'm okay with that. This one I find particularly interesting because it doesn't make sense. You've made sure that I always let Mom take the lead. She sets out the plan and I go with it. I don't try to convince her of anything. I don't try to correct her. I take the path of least resistance and go along with whatever she's presenting.

Lawrence, on the other hand, is the one who tries to give her direction, insisting she deal with business like banking and bills.

With me, she's mature and tries to maintain control. With Lawrence, she often acts like a little girl, pouty or giggling, as the case may be.

In any case, my brother sure is getting the excitement this time around!

Lawrence came upstairs, looking somewhat more relaxed and comfortable in old sweat pants and a flannel pullover. He thanked me for the ice cream.

"You're making me crazy," I burst out as he calmly spooned the creamy vanilla into his mouth. "Come on. What happened next?"

"Patience, Sister." I could tell he was feeling better, taunting me the way he had when we were kids. Always self-controlled, he had made sure his Halloween candy lasted a month, while mine was gone in a day. I wanted things to happen immediately. Lawrence patiently took his time. Then, like now, I knew I couldn't hurry him, but it didn't stop me from trying.

"Blood and Money, Part Two," I urged.

He set his empty dish aside and took up the tale once again. "I did not know I had committed a grievous sin until I was informed of such."

"What sin?"

"Taking Father to Calgary with me. Mother knows I always see Father when I come down, but this was the first time I took him anywhere. I drive her places. I take her shopping. I take her out for dinner. I stay at her place. Father? I take him for breakfast the day I'm leaving. I guess this has always been a source of pride for her, that I spend more time with her than with him. Consequently, my taking him down south resulted in serious resentment on Mom's part.

"So we're in this blood bath and I'm trying to make some order of it all. I wipe up blood. I insist Mom sit down on the chair. I clean up one area while she berates me for going out of my way to do favours for Father. Each time she gets worked up, her nose starts to bleed again. Up she leaps, looking for more tissue. I talk her down, tell her to sit quietly, lean her head back. She settles for a bit. I go clean some more; she starts talking and gets worked up. Finally, I took her to the bedroom and insisted she lie down and rest."

"And she gave in?"

"She did, but not easily. I think she saw I wasn't going to put up with any guff. I got her settled with a magazine and went back to finish wiping the kitchen, the bathroom, the floors. It took about an hour and by then she was sound asleep. I wasn't going to disturb her."

"Well, now I know the 'Blood' part of the story. Where does the money come in?"

Lawrence took a deep breath and huffed a dramatic sigh. I didn't begrudge his theatrics. This had truly been quite the event.

"When I cleaned Mom's table I found a number of bills. Some appeared to be paid, some weren't. A few had reminder notes to pay in the future. And that two thousand dollars? Still sitting there. She must have been trying to organize it again. Twenties were in various piles. Fifties separated out. She'd put some of the cash in the envelopes with the bills. It was total confusion."

"I've been wondering for a long time how she's been managing her bills," I said. "Were any badly overdue?"

"None that I could see. But she'd written questions on some of the envelopes. The guy that shovels her sidewalks in the winter? He'd sent a final bill for $645. She'd written on that envelope: 'Why are you charging me so much money? Can you prove I owe this to you?' That sort of thing."

"Poor Mom. She was always so confident in managing her affairs. I'm pretty sure that snow removal bill is accurate, though. We had four snowstorms in February and another in March. Her walks were always done when I came to visit. She's used him for years. I can't see him ripping her off."

"That was my thought, too. Anyway, it was clear she needed help to sort out the bills and money and all. I could hear her snoring, so I got to work. I organized the papers, made a list of the bills that were paid so she could refer to it and know what was completed, and filed those bills in her "Paid" shoe box. Then I made a list of anything outstanding along with the due date, and clipped those bills to it. I divided the cash into ten envelopes of two hundred dollars each. Everything was sorted when she got up. Her nose had stopped bleeding. The house no longer looked like a scene from a slasher movie. I expected she'd be grateful to wake up to calm and order, especially when I showed her the financial stuff was taken care of."

"You always were the practical one," I commented, but I was pretty sure I knew how this was going to turn out. Lawrence carried on with his sad tale.

"Whether it was the stress of the day, loss of blood, or her jealousy because I took Father to Calgary, I don't know, but she spiralled into a state of paranoia like I've never seen. Nothing I could say or do would distract her.

"Earlier, she'd said you were the bossy one. I was still in her favour. Not anymore. Apparently now we're both liars. We're robbing her blind. She rattled off accusations like she'd rehearsed them a dozen times. No struggle to find the words. No hesitation whatsoever. I've never felt like such a criminal. She even said the police had been alerted."

"She called the police?"

"No. I think it was part of the scenario she's been imagining. She was definitely trying to intimidate me like she did when we were kids.

I recognized the tone. Felt like I was twelve years old, getting caught stealing raspberries from the neighbour's yard.

"I was remorseful back then, but I wasn't today. That made her even angrier. Finally she hollered at me to leave her house *right now!* I tried a calm approach, to give her time to settle down, but that only seemed to make her anger escalate."

"So, once again, you've been banished?"

"Once again. Banished. Like a common criminal." He sighed and rose. "Time for bed. I'll probably head out early, so I'll say goodbye now. Thanks for letting me crash here."

"Any time. You know you're always welcome."

We hugged and Lawrence made his way downstairs.

I felt so badly for my big brother. If ever there was anyone who acts with absolute integrity, it's Lawrence—especially when it comes to Mom and her affairs.

Lawrence saw her need and thought his actions would be welcome. When it came time to explain, though, his logic couldn't penetrate her brain.

Complying with her uncompromising dismissal was the only option. He and I tease each other about how we justify backing off from Mom when we feel the need to do so. It's the only way to protect our sanity at times. His trigger points are different from mine, so what overwhelms him is often something I can tolerate; what overwhelms me is often something he can manage. I'm grateful neither of us berates the other for having to step back and regroup.

❦

Lord, please encourage Lawrence through all this. He's trying to be the best son he can be. He's doing things that would have pleased Mom in the past. Now it keeps backfiring. He must feel at such a loss when she's accusatory or just plain mean.

I don't believe it affects me to the same degree. As the black sheep of the family, the worst was always expected of me. Now that I'm her helper,

Mom justifies it by treating me as paid help, giving me twenty dollars when I take her for groceries. She wants my support, but seems to feel it's only acceptable if she pays me.

Through scripture, I understand that I'm to have a servant heart. My obedience in helping Mom is honouring to you, Jesus. No matter how Mom reacts, I know that ultimately I'm serving you. In this, I find fulfillment. Lawrence doesn't have that assurance, though. That makes it doubly hard for him, I think.

Lord, I pray that both Mom and Lawrence will one day find a relationship with you.

The Lost House

$\mathcal{I}$t was one of those rare afternoons when Rick and I were both home, both awake, and free to do what we wanted. On a whim, we decided to explore the organized chaos of architectural treasures at the new Habitat for Humanity ReStore shop that had opened nearby.

I was on my knees in a dusty corner, digging out a box of particularly attractive floor tiles when my cell phone rang. Tipping back onto my heels, I pulled the phone out of my pocket. Call display showed it was our daughter, Draya.

"Hey sweetie. What's up?" I expected she needed a quick favour. Given her condition of quadriplegia, Rick and I shared responsibility with her husband for managing some of her needs. She often called to ask if we could pick something up for her, or to ask us to swing by and attend to some small task. This time she took me by surprise.

"Grandma just called. She sounded pretty upset. She wanted me to find you and ask you to go over there. Right away."

My stomach clenched and fell simultaneously, if that's possible. This unexpected contact from Mom stirred up my usual feeling of anxiety but this time disappointment and a burst of resentment were layered with my anxiety. Rick and I would have to cut short our afternoon together.

"Did she say why?" I asked.

"I couldn't make out any reason, but she was clear that you have to go there right now."

"Okey-doke. Thanks for passing on the message."

Working my way up off the floor, I wondered. *Has Mom ever phoned Draya before? Maybe to say thank you for a birthday or Christmas card, but outside of that, I don't think so. This has to be serious. Okay, Lord. I'm giving you the resentment. If Mom needs me, she needs me. I'm trusting you to find another time for Rick and me to hang out. Now, where did that man get to?*

I searched up and down aisles lined with doors, cabinets, appliances, windows and a myriad of other demolition flotsam until I located Rick happily digging through a pile of electrical fixtures.

I rubbed his shoulder, getting his attention. He looked up, coming out of his reverie.

"Mom has an emergency,"

"What kind of emergency?"

"No idea. She called Draya and told her to find me and send me over there right away."

"Alrighty then." Rick replaced the jumble of connectors he'd been inspecting. I thanked God for a husband willing to change direction at a moment's notice.

"Do you want me to come with you?" he asked.

"Hmm…no. Stick around the phone, though. I'll call if we need you."

I dropped Rick at home and high-tailed it over to Mom's, rattling off random non-specific prayers as I drove. Fifteen minutes later I was knocking on her door.

Mom appeared calm and was formally polite as she ushered me in, but there was a tension I hadn't seen before. As usual, her radio was blaring out a local all-talk station, not quite tuned in. Static mingled with the commentator's voice.

"You'll be here," she said as I followed her into the kitchen. "There just isn't any way."

"Shall I make some tea?" I asked, falling back on the familiar.

"Of course you should. You have to know. I wouldn't have it away."

Mom's words were definitely confused. Plugging in the kettle and taking mugs from the cupboard gave me a moment to send up another quick prayer. *Lord, everything appears fine, but clearly it's not. Please help me to decipher what she's saying. At least give me the topic.* Mom took a jar of canned milk from the fridge and set it on the table beside the pink-flowered sugar bowl, a link to my childhood. Conversation was set aside as we carried out the mundane tasks that seemed to help ground Mom when things had gone sideways in her world.

"Can I turn the radio off?" I asked. Mom looked askance, as though she wasn't fully aware that the radio was on. After a moment she reached over and switched it off.

I relished the silence as we sat, watching the tea steep in our individual mugs.

Lord, this is definitely another one of those moments where Mom calls and my job is to show up, wait and listen. The rest is up to you and her. Please help Mom to find the words to explain what's happened. Help me grasp what's going on, and what, if anything, I need to do.

I added canned milk to both of our mugs, a little sugar in mine. I stirred and set the spoon aside. We sipped, neither speaking. The house was quiet. I waited.

Suddenly, with unexpected forcefulness, Mom spoke. "I had a blank today. Just…blank. I was, you know. I was, but it was blank. I was blank."

My mind formulated a dismissive reply, *We all have times like that,* but the Lord kept my mouth shut. To fill the silence, I took another sip of tea. Mom stared at the eyelet lace curtain, yellowed with age, which hung across the bottom half of the kitchen window. She sighed a shuddering breath. Emphatically, she spoke.

"Now I know why old people go out and wander and can't get home. Here. I was here. But I didn't know in my head the outside. I couldn't have found it. I know I couldn't. It wasn't there. In my head." Her words stumbled to a halt, her forehead furrowed.

"Do you mean you lost your memory of what your house looked like from the outside?"

"Yes!" She lit up.

Thank you, Lord, for this quick understanding. How frustrating it must be for Mom when she can only move fragments of thought from her brain to her tongue.

Mom's words flowed again.

"Yes!" she repeated. "If I'd gone out, I would not have found my way back. I could have frozen in the cold. I don't want to be that old fool on the news and all the neighbours beating the bushes looking for the geezer."

Lord, I don't think Mom is as frightened of being lost as she is of the potential humiliation of having her picture broadcast for all to see. Was it the prospect of being shamed that moved her to phone for help? Having her name splashed across the news, strangers searching for her and maybe finding her would be unbearable for someone as private as Mom.

"Do you remember your house now?" I asked.

"It happens. Anytime now. There's a point, always. What if I go out?"

I took that to mean she was still drawing a blank.

Suddenly the Lord spoke through my mouth. I knew it was Jesus, because the suggestion was as foreign to my relationship with Mom as anything I could imagine.

"Would you like to come to my house?" I asked. "You could come for a sleepover and tomorrow we could go shopping."

I was startled as I listened to my words, but at the same time, I was sure Mom would refuse the invitation. In her social economy, she would see herself as a burden, with no way to repay the favour. Mom was not experiencing her normal state of mind, however, and I was unprepared for her response.

Setting her mug firmly on the table, she launched into a list of sleepover ground rules. Had she considered this option already? I had no idea.

"You'll have to not get upset if I get mean and angry. When your brother was here I had a nosebleed. He was so good. He was so patient. I wasn't patient back. So if I get angry it's okay for us to fight. It doesn't mean anything. You can get angry and then get over it."

Hesitantly, I agreed. "Sure, Mom. If you get angry, I won't take it personally."

That settled, we again sat quietly. Our tea was cold, the house silent.

Lord, how in the world did you manage this? A sleepover? At our house? This is out of character for both of us. What am I supposed to do with her? What about work tomorrow? What about... My mind began to whirl until I was pulled up short with a sudden childhood recollection of summer holidays and long trips in the car. *I'm going on a trip and I'm going to pack...*

Oh! Of course. Thank you, Lord.

"I guess you'll need to pack a few things for overnight," I suggested, taking my cue from this divine revelation. In a certain amount of shock myself, my mind seemed to be as blank as Mom's. I thought back to several weeks ago when the plan for Mom to move into the basement had been a vague concept somewhere in the future, dependent on us building a bathroom. A sleepover today was much more immediate.

Lord, is this going to be a one-night visit, or will Mom stay longer? Is she going to move into the basement now, with the lovely little bathroom you gave us? Mom doesn't seem to be making any effort to pack. We can't sit here all day. If this is going to happen, help us figure out the logistics, please.

"Well," I said, "let's see what you want to take."

Mom followed obediently as I went to the bedroom. I had never before attempted to maintain someone's dignity while rifling through their unmentionables.

"Do you want to take these panties, or those ones?" I asked.

No response.

"What do you like to sleep in?"

Still nothing.

Mom stood by the bed, stroking the quilt serenely as she watched my actions. She seemed detached, as though she was gazing out a window. The more I tried to include her, the more distant she became. Finally she moved to the dresser.

"This is your mail," she told me, holding up a large plastic freezer bag.

"No, that's your mail, Mom. I don't think we need to take that."

"Did your brother want it? I haven't asked him. Do you know? We have to keep all the pieces together."

Lord, I remember how upset she became with Lawrence when he tried to help. I don't want to get Mom worked up and have her feel she can't come to our house. At the same time, I need to know things I don't know. I can't believe I'm asking you, Jesus, but can you tell me, please? What bra does Mom wear? Does she sleep in this old nightie or that one? Her underwear is an amazing variety of sizes. I don't know if she wears the extra-large, large, or medium. Cotton or nylon? Do I ask? Or do I just gather one of everything?

Leaving Mom in the bedroom, I escaped the surreal endeavour and went to the basement in search of a small overnight bag. Several large suitcases, circa 1950, were piled in a corner of the suite. I dismissed a hard, square cosmetic case from the top of the pile. After checking the clasps on the various pieces of luggage, I finally chose a large red suitcase. *Don't let me pack it too heavy, Lord. Suitcases didn't have wheels when these were made. I don't want to strain my back!*

I dragged the scarlet monstrosity into the bedroom. I felt as though I were on stage, performing a one-woman monologue as I continued to pose questions to this unresponsive audience of one. Eventually I gave up and gathered anything that looked like it might be used on a regular basis. I closed the suitcase and snapped the clasps in place.

"Ready?" I asked. Mom smiled a tourist smile and followed the monstrosity and me to the front closet. I moved her jackets back and forth on the rail, waiting for her to choose one. She smiled, as unwilling to take part in the conversation of "It's cold and I'm going to wear..." as she had been in, "I'm going on a trip and I'm going to pack..."

Taking a pink, sporty looking car-coat, I handed it to her.

"Is this one okay?"

"I haven't worn that for ages. Where in the world did you find it?"

"Right here. Do you want this one or a different one?" We were back to the smile. "This one should do," I answered myself. "I'll carry it for you."

Suddenly Mom's brain switched back on. "Are we taking your little car? Do you think I might drive it? Just a little ways. I do miss driving. That was terrible the way they took away my license. Do you know how terrible it is not to drive?"

Chatting like a magpie, Mom followed me as I braced the crimson monster against my hip and bumped down the steps. I settled Mom in the car, then heaved the suitcase into the trunk.

Keys. The house wasn't locked.

"Do you have your keys, Mom?"

"Keys?"

Mom stroked the dash lovingly. "You have such a beautiful car," she said wistfully. "It's so clean! I miss driving." Leaving Mom in my dusty little Kia, I zipped back into the house, found her keys on the end table and locked the deadbolt. I paused. Unlocking the door, I went into the kitchen—burners off; the bathroom—taps off; the bedroom—lights off...

Oh my. I'm getting as bad as Mom. Is she really coming to sleep over at my house, Lord? Has that ever happened since I left home over forty years ago?

Nope. Never.

So be it. You're in charge, Lord. Take it away!

Sleepover

*A*s we drove to my house, Mom kept up a running commentary: "The trees are so green."

"How can there be so many cars?"

"Are you still working with children?"

"Look at the buildings. I don't have any idea where we are."

I wasn't very attentive, I'm afraid. My thoughts were churning. *What should our next step be? Should Mom sleep in the basement suite? After all, that was the plan just a couple of months ago. The bed's made up. The bathroom is ready to use. But is that really wise? What if she has another blank moment and leaves the house through the back door? What if she suddenly remembers her house and goes looking for it? We might not hear her. No. Upstairs feels safer.*

I pressed 'pause' on my runaway thoughts as we pulled into the driveway. Mom and I and the red monstrosity of a suitcase entered the door just as Rick was coming into the kitchen. He looked a little startled.

"Mom's coming for a sleepover!" I announced enthusiastically.

"Great idea," Rick said with a grin, taking Mom's suitcase from me. I appreciated how he could roll with the waves and barely acknowledge that the ship was rocking violently.

I was torn between keeping Mom company in the living room and setting up a bed for her. *What if she comes to herself and decides she's a burden? After all this, what if she decides she wants to go home? I know, Lord. I'm over-thinking. Help me take one minute at a time.*

"Here, Mom, why don't you sit in the comfy recliner? There, I'll put the footrest up." *This way it will be harder for her to get out of it while I'm out of the room.* Handing her the local paper, I scurried away, taking Rick with me to the downstairs storage room.

"So, how did this come about?" he asked when we were out of earshot.

I gave him a quick rundown.

"How long will she stay?" he asked.

"Your guess is as good as mine, but I want her upstairs, just to be safe."

He nodded as he pulled some bins and boxes out of the way. Together we dragged a twin-sized mattress up the stairs, trying not to be obvious about it. Knowing my mother as I do, I kept waiting for reality to kick in. *When will she notice how much work we're going to and decide she's too much trouble? I can't believe this scenario has played out this long! Except for short visits with planned escapes, Mom never enters someone else's world. Where is the mother I've known all these years? Who is this woman who has replaced her?*

Rick and I arranged a bed in my sewing room. I stood back and surveyed the impromptu bedroom—one more scene in this very strange play. To create a platform for the mattress, we'd placed a sheet of plywood on four large Rubbermaid bins. Mattress, sheets and a blue flowered quilt made an inviting bed. Mom's suitcase was open on my sewing table. A lamp stood on a folding TV tray by the bed, along with a couple of magazines. Mom had always read before she went to sleep. I assumed she still did.

Mom's tranquility continued through the evening. We had a light supper and watched the news. A copy of *Maclean's* magazine in hand, she settled on the couch, turning sideways and putting her feet up, as though this were the most natural thing ever. I had to consciously refrain from shaking my head.

As she read, I stole a few moments to send a quick email to several on our church prayer team. "My mother seems to have lost her memory of her own house. I've brought her to my place to sleep over tonight. No idea where this is going. Please pray!" No further explanation was required. We had been praying for Mom's situation for over a year, so everyone understood the circumstances.

"What are we doing here?" she asked suddenly, looking up from the magazine.

"Just relaxing for the evening," I responded. I didn't know whether I should allude to the precipitous event of forgetting her house or not.

"Do you see this?" Mom indicated a headline promoting an upcoming Children's Festival. "They do this all the time. No one learns. They really should, though. They won't get away with it for long."

"No, they won't," I responded. Mom's conversation was coming out as a series of phrases, with no discernible subject matter. Joining her where she was at and going with the flow seemed the easiest approach.

"We're in your house, aren't we."

"Yes, we are."

"Look at this. If they ever had money. They won't get away with it. They ought to be careful. People know."

For the next little while Mom shared her incomprehensible insights into the stories behind the headlines, and I readily agreed with whatever opinion she tried to express.

"Could I have a drink?"

"Sure. Would you like tea? Juice?"

"Tea would be nice."

The evening wore on and Mom's contentment persisted. I could not recall any time in our history where she'd been so calm. Headlines that normally raised her ire received simple observations. She continued to chat on random topics, interspersed with wistful comments relating to her sorrow at no longer being able to drive. She rambled on as though our evening together was perfectly normal. She asked for another drink. Even that was remarkable. Mom never asked for anything when she was a guest somewhere. This time I gave her some juice. Perhaps all her talking was making her thirsty.

Mom finally reached the end of the magazine and closed it up. She raised her head and looked about the room expectantly. *Lord, I don't have the energy to try to engage in Mom's convoluted conversations right now. What can we do for the rest of the evening?*

Grabbing the remote, I scrolled through a few channels. Mom is not a television watcher so I was pleased when I found a documentary on sea life that caught her attention.

"What a beautiful picture!" she addressed Rick. "What a fine machine you have. You know so much about these things. I can't believe you know how to make this work."

As sea life swam across the screen, I pondered Mom's comment back at her house— that we'd have to be patient if we got mean or angry. There didn't seem to be any worry about that now.

Around nine-thirty, Mom announced in a genial tone that she was off to bed. Like a mother hen, I followed her down the hallway, pointing out the obvious. I had no idea how much she was taking in, or whether it even mattered.

"Here's your magazine, Mom. I'll turn on the lamp for you so you can read in bed. This is how you turn it off. See the switch? Here's your suitcase. Your nightie is on the bed. And your housecoat. The bathroom is right next door, to the left when you come out of the room. Rick and I are right across the hall. You can call out if you need anything."

Mom stood quietly as I rattled off my list, a tranquil expression adorning her face.

Lord, this feels so unnatural! I don't believe I've ever seen my mother at peace before. Firm, constrained, determined, controlled, but never at peace. Seeing this contrast, I'm realizing that she's always been anxious around others. I've always responded to that with wariness, walking on eggshells. You'd think I'd enjoy this turn of events, but I have to admit, I'm even more cautious. Is she going to explode at some point?

When I could think of no more instructions, I asked, "Do you want the door closed?"

"Yes." She walked into the bedroom, turned, and smiled sweetly one more time. "Good night," she called pleasantly as she shut the door.

I was still in shock. *A sleepover with a peaceful mother who is open to being taken care of? This is surreal. Does she really know where she is? Does she perhaps believe she's in a hotel? She certainly doesn't appear to believe she's staying at her daughter's house.* The sensation remained that we were acting in some bizarre play.

I wasn't about to keep this experience to myself. Lawrence was the only other person who would understand how out of character Mom was behaving, so I called him long distance and shared the details of this very odd day. I'm not sure he believed me, but at least I could debrief a little.

After we said good-bye I sent a quick email, notifying my boss that I wouldn't be in the next day. *Thank you, Lord, that I work for a company that understands sometimes family must take precedence over the job.*

Finally I crawled into my own bed, wondering whether Mom would sleep through the night. I said a quick prayer, placing her in the Lord's hands, and closed my eyes.

Rick and I heard nothing through the night.

At seven-thirty Mom was still in bed. I checked my emails. My boss Janet had replied, giving me her blessing to take a personal day. I ended my morning devotions with a prayer. *Lord, I haven't heard a peep. Is she still with us? Perhaps I'll make another pot of coffee and then look in on her. Please guide me through this day. I'm at a real loss to know what to do.*

When I opened the sewing room door, Mom was sleeping on her side. The lamp beside her makeshift bed still burned brightly. Her face, creased with skin too loose for her skull, looked vulnerable without her glasses. As I stared, her eyes suddenly opened, and she looked directly at me.

"Good morning," I said brightly, not sure what to expect. "Would you like a cup of coffee?"

"Oh yes. Coffee. I slept all night. I don't know when I've slept so well!"

"I'm glad! I'll have the coffee ready when you come out. All your clothes are in your suitcase there on the sewing table."

Twenty minutes later Mom joined me in the kitchen, dressed in slacks and a blouse, hair brushed, glasses in place. In contrast to my continued bewilderment, Mom appeared strong, secure and comfortable. As we shared the freshly brewed coffee, I offered suggestions for the day.

"I don't need to work today, so we can shop if you want to, and have lunch at the mall."

"That's good. I need to shop. I have nothing to cover my bottom," she giggled.

Whole wheat toast and jam would make for a simple breakfast. I poured us each a second cup of coffee.

As I waited for the toast to pop, my mind was darting every which way. *Lord, how do I broach the subject of where she plans to sleep tonight? Do I ask if she wants to stay over again? Do I ask if she wants to stay forever, since last night went so nicely? And she slept so well. Is it because she's in a place where your Spirit lives? If I ask her to stay and she agrees, how will I acclimatize her to the house and still go to work? If she wants to go home, will she be able to manage there? Does she remember her house now?*

In my heart I felt an emphatic, yet gentle, statement: Be still. And know that I am God.

I chuckled. *Right. Okay. I can do that.*

I brought our toast and coffee to the living room. I was in need of a third-party distraction, so I turned the television on. Mom watched the morning news. I surreptitiously watched Mom as she continued to behave as though we were playing parts in a delightful stage production. How I wished I could settle in and enjoy myself as much as Mom seemed to, but I had no confidence that this would last. Once again, I felt out of my depth, but this time, because things were going too well.

After washing up, we drove to the mall. Mom explored the racks of underwear for a short time, but tired quickly. We stopped for an early lunch at Albert's Restaurant.

"We should share an omelet," Mom decided. "I could never eat a whole one!"

However, she insisted we order two large slices of lemon meringue pie. "You'll want your own," she admonished when I suggested we share dessert as well.

Midafternoon found us back at my house. As Mom sat and stroked Maggie, I decided to approach my quandary in the simplest way possible.

"What would you like to do now?"

"Well, we need to be in our own home, you know. I can't be a burden on you."

Not a burden, but certainly a complication! This sounds more like the mother I know. Is she coming back to herself?

I sensed we were returning to familiar ground and pursued Mom's state of mind a little further. "Do you feel comfortable being back at your house?"

"Why wouldn't I?"

I hesitated, then made a quick decision. *I'll let yesterday's selective amnesia remain in the past.*

Mom watched without comment as I packed her things into the great red suitcase. The drive to her house was relatively quiet. We made small talk as I returned her clothes and toiletries to the locations in which I'd found them. My wariness continued as I waited for her to raise a ruckus about this violation of privacy. The tongue-lashing she'd given Lawrence was still fresh in my mind. It didn't seem to be an issue today, however. For that, I was grateful.

"When will you need groceries?" I asked as I was leaving.

"Oh, I'll give you a call. I have plenty. You really don't need to be worrying about me all the time, you know. I manage just fine. Just fine."

On that note we hugged. Relieved, I made my exit.

⚬⚭⚬

Lord, is your light what Mom feels when she comes to our house? When she looked at the basement two months ago, she seemed overcome with joy and a desire to live here. She seemed to feel safe, welcome. But when she left, she turned away from that welcome, and reclaimed her own home, a familiar place, even though it frightens her. Yesterday when she slept over she was again calm and peaceful, even in the midst of disrupted memory and broken brain waves. Is it you she's experiencing? Is she feeling the Holy Spirit in this place? It seems the spiritual battle within her is part of what causes such dissension with Lawrence and me.

John 1:5 says; "The light shines in the darkness, and the darkness has not overcome it."

Darkness cannot overcome the light, but people can, if we choose to. We can come into your light, bask in it, enjoy it, and feel blessed in it. Yet with free will, we can turn and walk away, back into darkness. Why do we do that, Lord? It makes no sense that we can find a place of peace, acknowledge how wonderful it feels, and then turn away again. Do we think we can take the peace with us? Do we think we can have this gift separate from you?

It's like tasting sweet milk, and then putting it down to go and drink bitter, brackish water. Why do we continue to crave our familiar, destructive ways?

The darkness has not overcome the light, nor will it, but the darkness remains. People hover at the edge of your light, as though they were vampires afraid of the sun.

What's wrong with us, Lord? Your promises are huge, your provision abundant. Yet, afraid of being constrained by your moral law, most prefer the meagre existence of "my will" to "thy will."

How does this understanding fit with my relationship with Mom? As always, I guess it comes down to the basics. Am I being fully obedient? I want to be totally in, no-holds-barred. Your will and yours alone. I'm trusting you to show me the way in which I should go, the way you choose. And I pray that even in her state of dementia, Mom will be drawn to you.

Strategies

Sunday was cold. Promises of spring had disappeared as wind slashed across the streets and yards. Snow scurried over freshly shovelled sidewalks. Rick groaned as he gazed out the living room window, reconciling himself to the fact that he'd be shovelling again before the day was out.

I happily assumed the role of housewife. Dinner simmering in the crockpot, tea steaming at my right hand, I prepared to spend the afternoon curled up in my rocker, organizing family photos on my laptop. I like shovelling snow sometimes but on cold blustery days I'm happy to leave it to Rick.

Christmas was long gone so it was certainly time to tackle this project. As I labeled and sorted the family photos I was suddenly struck with inspiration. *Photos! Mom needs a page of photos with all the family members on one sheet of paper and our names underneath. Then she can review it at her leisure and remind herself who's who.*

This new project grabbed my full attention as I set to work cropping and pasting headshots of Lawrence, his kids and grandkids, me and my husband and kids into a Word document on my laptop. I pasted them in family groups, typed their names in a large font, noting who was married to whom, and added their phone numbers as an extra help.

At one point, Rick poked his head into the living room. "Is the food in the crockpot ready?"

I glanced at the clock. "Oh! Yes! Definitely. Just let me finish this bit and I'll be right there..."

Some time later I discovered a bowl of stew sitting beside me. A glance into the kitchen revealed that my dear hubby had put the rest of the stew in plastic containers, ready for meals through the coming week. I called out a heartfelt "Thank you!" and carried on with my project.

I was yawning by the time I printed off two copies of my creative rendering. I tucked them into my purse and headed off to bed, pleased with the fruits of my labour.

Lord, thanks for the great idea. I hope Mom likes it as much as I do. I'm taking her shopping tomorrow. It would help if you could prepare her mind so she can grasp how to use the photos as a reference sheet. I'll leave that in your hands. Thanks, again.

The next day the wind had abated. I called Mom from work, just to be sure she remembered we were going to shop. When I arrived she was dressed and ready to leave. I parked by Safeway, but treats came first so we made our way down the mall.

"Coffee and pie will give sustenance for our to-do list," Mom announced. I laughed, happy to agree to her plan. We chatted amiably while we enjoyed apple pie à la mode, and several refills of coffee.

"What's next on your list, Mom?" I asked as the server placed our bill on the table.

"I'm getting this," she said as she dug into her purse. I checked the bill. $13.45.

"Do you have a ten and a five? That will cover it."

Mom rummaged some more. She pulled a fistful of papers from her purse and placed them on the table.

"How do people keep track?" she muttered. I waited. Patiently. Next, her little black wallet came out. She unzipped it and began pushing the accordion-style flaps back and forth, moving folded bills in the process. I wanted to reach over and pull out the cash, but restrained myself. *Lord, let me be patient and allow Mom as much time as she needs.*

"That was lovely pie, but I don't know how they can keep doing it. It's not going to continue. I just know."

I watched as the wallet found its way back into her purse, still holding the cash.

"Here's the bill, Mom," I hinted, nudging the register slip a little closer. "Do you want me to cover it today? You can get it next time."

She looked at the bill, frowning. The wad of papers from her purse regained her attention.

"The bill? Oh yes. Here it is."

She pulled an old Visa statement from the pile and laid it on the table. Pointing to the dollar sign by the *Amount Due* box, she asked, "Do you think this is enough to cover it? It should be enough."

"Yes, that's just right," I said, relieved to have a way out of the moment. It crossed my mind that some might construe this as lying, but as my patience was now wearing thin, I pushed that thought away. "Have you got your coat there?"

Mom's attention moved to her coat and gloves, and I slipped a twenty out of my wallet, placing it on the table under the bill. Then I secreted the Visa statement in my pocket. Judging by its worn edges, it had been living in Mom's purse for quite some time. I doubted it was outstanding. In any case, another statement would arrive at some point. I was simply happy we could escape the restaurant and carry on about our business.

Mom consulted her little piece of paper before heading into the mall. "Stamps. I need stamps. Is there a post office here?

"We can stop at the drug store. They have a post office in the back."

"Oh my. Is it a long way away? I don't know that I can walk a long way today. My back you know…"

"It's on the way to Safeway," I reminded her. "Just a few stores down. Let me know if you want to sit and rest, though."

"I don't need to rest. I walk every day. You treat me like I'm old!"

I laughed. "You have great energy, Mom. I hope I have your determination when I'm your age."

"And well you should."

On that note, we stepped out.

I was pleased to see only one person in line at the post office counter. "Do you have your letters with you?" I asked, remembering seeing several fresh, clean envelopes when Mom had pulled her papers out in the restaurant.

"I do. I do." The wad returned to the light of day and I helped Mom separate three letters from the old, tattered pile. I checked the addresses surreptitiously, noting they looked complete. The little black wallet came out and, once again, Mom shuffled its accordion folds. The letters and tattered pile returned to her purse. At least we knew where they were, though.

"It's our turn, Mom." I took her by the arm and gently directed her attention to the clerk. By now three people were lined up behind us. I knew I shouldn't feel pressured, but I wanted to at least try to be efficient in our transactions.

"I'd like stamps," Mom said clearly.

"Yeah, okay. How many." The young clerk's bored expression reflected no hint of urgency. I decided if the clerk didn't feel the need to hurry, then neither would I. Letting Mom carry out her business, I stepped back a little and waited.

"How many can I have?"

"As many as you want. They come in packets of ten or thirty or a roll of a hundred."

"A hundred? Oh no. I don't need that many. I'd be dead before I used them all!" Mom chuckled at her little joke and looked endearingly at the clerk.

The clerk stared blankly. "So, how many?"

Mom turned to me. "What do you think?"

"How about ten for now? We can always get more, if you need them."

"Do you think that's enough? What if it snows and I can't get out again?"

The line behind us was growing. I could now feel five pairs of eyes boring into our backs.

"If it snows, I can pick up more for you after work."

"But then you'd have to drive on the bad roads. That's not safe."

"We'll take ten," I said to the clerk pleasantly, keeping any hint of frustration out of my voice. I might have succeeded in that. However, my quick grab for a ten dollar bill from Mom's wallet revealed my growing irritation. The clerk conducted our transaction, and I led Mom to the side so she could sort her change.

"I have three letters," she announced as she put the coins into her wallet, slowly dividing nickels, dimes and quarters into their respective folds.

"Do you have them there?"

She carefully pulled the letters from the pile, laying each on the side counter. Next she neatly tucked and re-tucked the wad of papers into her purse, then took them out again, shuffled through the pile, returned them, took them out once more, turned them around and put them back.

Breathe. Breathe. Wait. No rush.

Now she turned to the packet of stamps and began to fumble with the cover. After several false starts she managed to open it, and then tried to hook the first stamp with her fingernail. Over and over, she flicked and scratched at it with no success.

"Here, I can help, Mom." She had often told me how her fingertips were numb. It seemed reasonable that I assist.

I quickly placed three stamps on three letters and popped them into the slot under the counter. Mom put the rest of the stamps in her purse. I was careful not to make eye contact with any of the now-seven people lined up as we left the counter.

I did hear Mom, though, as she quietly said, "I hope I can remember that the letters got mailed, since I didn't do it myself."

Oh, Lord, I never thought of that. Good intentions aside, help is not always help, is it? With dementia, it makes sense that a memory is more likely to be built if Mom carries out the action herself. And yes, I was getting a little impatient. Please help me take the time Mom needs.

When we reached Safeway, Mom was struggling to keep up the pace.

"Shall we get your milk and bread later?" I asked. "You still have some in the fridge. I think you'll be okay until the weekend."

"I'm certainly not going to get groceries today," she agreed. Relieved, we made our way to the car and drove back to her house.

Mom put on the kettle, and I put tea bags into our mugs. Mom took evaporated milk stored in an old Miracle Whip jar from the fridge. I found the sugar, just a little crusted over. I wondered whether Mom was too tired to absorb my Family Tree idea, but at least it was something to talk about. As we sipped our tea, I brought out my page of pictures.

"Take a look at this, Mom."

"What nice looking people," she peered with interest. "Who are they?"

"Well, this is Lawrence. Here's his name under the photo. And his phone number." I pointed. Mom peered closer. "And here's his son, Shaemus, and Shaemus' wife Joanne. Here are their children..." Bit by bit we worked through the family tree and talked about each person.

"I thought you could keep this handy," I suggested, "so if you forget someone's name, you could refer to it."

"Is this your boy? What's his name?"

"That's Luke. Your grandson."

"Is this your girl? What's her name?"

"That's Draya. And this is her husband..." We worked through the pictures and names once more.

"If you keep the page on your table," I tried again, "you can check it and remember who's who in the family."

"They're very nice-looking people. Do you know who they are? Here. Have some more tea."

"No, thanks," I demurred. *I'm managing to maintain my patience, and I thank you for that, Lord. But this great idea feels mighty pointless. What was I thinking?*

"I need to take the garbage out." Mom stood, but then paused by the table, reaching for the page of pictures. "You know, I could use this to remember people's names. Who is that one there? See? It says 'Lawrence.' I'm going to keep this on the table here."

I felt a glimmer of hope. *Perhaps the concept has slipped into Mom's understanding after all.*

"There's a second copy too, Mom. You could keep this one in your purse."

"Well, you might lose your purse," Mom sputtered, appalled at my apparently ridiculous suggestion. "You shouldn't carry around private things like that for just anyone to get hold of!"

She's okay with carrying hundreds of dollars in cash when she goes out, but something identifying her or her family is a danger? I'm not even going to try to decipher her logic, Lord. I'll leave that with you.

Reasonable or not, prudence dictated that I adopt Mom's position. "No pictures in your purse. Very good."

I knew arguing or explaining rarely changed her thought process, and I had another idea in mind. I wondered if I could get her to agree. "Mom, remember when you said it was hard for you to remember your house and what it looks like?"

"I only live in one room now. I hate it. That bedroom. I can't go out of that room. The people are here."

"The people?" I asked. "What people?"

"At night. You know. But now I have to take the garbage to the alley," she stated firmly, reaching for her coat.

End of subject. Okay. Back to my own subject, then. "Mom, I have my camera here in my purse. Why don't I take a picture of you on the steps? Then you'll have a picture of you and your house so you can remember what it looks like."

"A picture? What a good idea! You're so smart!" she said, beaming and patting my arm.

I was completely taken aback. *Could it be that easy? No convoluted discussion? No refusal? Well, Hallelujah!*

We tied up Mom's garbage, buttoned her coat, and she slipped on her old outside shoes. Mom posed on the porch, looking strong and confident, and I snapped the photo.

Garbage bag in hand, Mom walked me to the car and waved as I pulled out, a smile lighting her face.

I breathed deeply, and then remembered her comment. "The people are there. At night."

People? What people? Ah well, if it's important, time will reveal it, I'm sure.

I wove my way through the six o'clock traffic, relieved to have survived another excursion into Mom's distinctive world.

Back home, I downloaded the picture onto my computer and printed it.

Nancy and her home of forty years

❧

I wonder if Mom will ever use this, Lord? In any case, I have a great photo of her and her beloved home, the physical representation of her independence these past forty years. What of the future, though? Sometimes I wonder if our efforts to keep her independent are a form of denial. The dementia marches forward, and nothing we do is going to stop it. We put in place different strategies, pretending they'll thwart the progression, but every time I visit, I see a greater loss of capacity. Does Mom see it too? Is she aware that she's getting worse?

Lord, part of me thinks I should call Lawrence and discuss forcing a move. But whenever I pray about it, you lay it on my heart that I need to wait. Wait for what? Are you going to allow her to die in her house? We don't know what her health is like. She hasn't seen a doctor in over a decade.

That feels morbid. Is it wrong of me to be thinking such things?

As usual, this is way out of my realm of understanding. Lord, I place Mom in your hands. My hope is that even with the dementia, you'll reach her mind, her heart, so she'll make a decision to accept you as her saviour.

In the meantime, I trust you to tell me, loud and clear, if I should be doing something differently. Until then, I guess it's status quo.

Is that even possible with dementia?

Sigh.

Chapter Seventeen

"Hello?"

Mom's childlike voice answered my call. She'd complained all her life that people thought she was a little girl when she spoke on the telephone. Even at ninety, that childlike quality remained. I'd been trying to call her on and off for the past few days. I was relieved now that she'd answered.

My relief was short-lived.

"Hi, Mom. It's Bobbi. How are you doing?"

"I'm surprised you actually called me," she sputtered.

"Mom, what's wrong?"

"Don't act like you don't know. You know very well"

"But I don't. Can you tell me what's happened?"

"You and your brother happened. That's what."

It's amazing how much fury she can put into her words, how articulate she is when she's angry. Lawrence thought his visit last week had gone well, but maybe not...Lord, help me understand what's going on.

"Did something happen when Lawrence was here?"

The sound of the radio blared from her kitchen, but it didn't cover the curse she uttered. "You're nothing but liars and stealers, the both of you."

"What was stolen?"

"You know very well what was stolen. The two of you are talking behind my back all the time, planning and manipulating. I know you have keys for this house."

"I do, Mom." I released my clenched jaw and paused to draw a calming breath. "You and I were at the mall when you said you wanted me to have a set of your keys for emergencies. Remember? We got them cut together."

"Liar! You're, both of you, deceivers." I heard spittle slap her receiver. "You and your brother are planning all this behind my back!"

"But, Mom, I haven't talked to Lawrence since he was here last weekend."

"That's one more lie. He just takes off and leaves *you* here." The way she said *you* made it clear Mom didn't think being left in my hands was anything to be desired. "You better watch it, you two," she added. "People are watching for this sort of thing. They'll find out. They'll see what you're doing."

"Mom, truly, I have no idea what you're talking about."

She cursed again and the phone went dead.

I imagined her pushing herself up from her old green chair and marching to the kitchen, huffing and fuming. As for me, I sat, stunned, not knowing what to do next. Reach out? Connect? Yes! When lost, confused and alone, turn to Facebook!

STATUS UPDATE:

Bobbi Junior, Monday, near Edmonton
I give up. Am I allowed to give up? How does one actually carry out giving up? I have no idea. I just give up.
LIKE. COMMENT. SHARE.

RICK JUNIOR
Depends! Whatcha giving up? If it's me…sorry, you're not allowed. If it's the kids…sorry, you're not allowed. If it's the day and it's late and you did good today…then yeah, you can give up! :)

That evening Rick joined me in the living room where I could vent in comfort.

"So what are you giving up?" He cranked the footrest of the La-Z-Boy to a reclining position and settled in while I processed my frustration out loud.

"Well, certainly not you," I chuckled, thinking of his Facebook reply. "And not the kids. But days like this, I sure wish I could back out of being Mom's tool for independence."

One grey bushy brow rose and his head tilted, inviting me to continue.

"She thinks Lawrence and I are stealing from her. I think the issue is coming from what Lawrence said he did with that two thousand dollars she took out of the bank. He put it in envelopes of two hundred dollars each, in the bottom of her lockbox. My guess is that she doesn't remember where it went.

"Mm-hmm…" Rick's a great listener.

"Whatever the reason, she's furious with both of us. She said we should be careful because people are watching for this kind of thing and they'll see what we're doing. I think she was referring to financial elder abuse. She said we've made keys to get into her house. Maybe she remembers me getting them cut, but not that it was her idea."

"She's read a lot about the scams con men pull on the elderly, hasn't she?"

"Oh my, yes. She'll buy any magazine that has an article about taking advantage of seniors. That knowledge is very strong in her mind. If she remembers getting the money when Lawrence was here, but she can't find it now, she must think those horror stories have become a reality. Lawrence and I are the culprits trying to steal from her.

"I tried to tweak her memory about getting the keys cut, hoping that would help. That's when she hung up.

"The other problem is that if I'm right, if she doesn't know where her money is, then she can't get groceries and she'll be getting low on food around now. If she won't talk to me, I can't tell her where Lawrence put it."

Rick, patient and wise, didn't offer any advice. Sometimes venting is all that's needed.

"So yeah," I concluded. "I give up…at least until Jesus shows me what to do next."

Lord, it's been three days now. I keep trying to think of reasons to call Mom. When I pray, though, I feel a barrier in my spirit. It's as if you're saying that calling might alleviate my worry, but it won't be in her best interest. As long as you're not giving me a sense of peace about making contact, I have to assume you're doing some work in her, and you need her to be on her own to move it forward. So, calling might make me feel better but it could prolong what you're trying to accomplish.

Am I reading this right? Sometimes I wish I could access your direction in a more concrete manner. I need one of those neon arrows saying, 'This way!' It's so hard to know if I'm hearing you correctly.

You've stopped me before, though, until the time was right. Then it felt very right.

Okay. I'm going to sit tight until you open the door for me to move. But, oh, the waiting is hard.

⸙

It's been ten days since that angry conversation, and no contact.

I'm reading John's Gospel. In chapter 19:9, Jesus refused to defend himself before Pilate and the chief priests, even though he knew they were preparing to crucify him.

I defended myself to Mom, telling her Lawrence and I hadn't talked about her. I defended myself again when I reminded her it was her idea to get another set of keys cut. That was when she hung up. Would the call have ended differently if I'd kept my own interests out of it, if I'd only spoken Jesus' love as I have in the past?

Lord, help me remember simply to listen, empathize and show your love. That seems to be what works best for Mom when she's upset.

But the cause of her anger is a concern, too. Is this conversation indicative of a further loss of rational thinking? The few professionals I've talked to about Mom's situation say she's at a stage where I should take charge and force her into assisted living. I'm afraid that if I did that we'd lose the fragile truce we have. If she can't trust me, she'll have no advocate. I can't do it, Lord. Until you tell me differently, I'm leaving Mom in your hands.

As for me, I'll wait on your direction. Please watch over her, and may your will be done.

Chapter Eighteen

Easter morning I wandered into the kitchen in search of coffee. Propped against the pot was a bright pink envelope, addressed to *My Wife*.

Shoot! He not only remembered, he remembered on time!

Rick and I are both forgetful when it comes to special occasions. Sometimes neither of us remembers until after the event. This time he'd won. I knew he would be insufferable... *Wait! If I'm quick...*

Rick was still asleep—his night shift guaranteed that. I threw on jeans and a sweatshirt and zipped over to the 24-hour drugstore.

Driving home, an appropriately romantic card stowed in my purse, my mind detoured from what had so far been a pleasant morning and stumbled onto the rocky path of worry.

Two weeks now and no contact with Mom. The break is welcome, Lord, but guilt abounds. Every day I practice your admonition to cast my care on you. Still, part of me wants to call, just to alleviate my concern. But when I consider making that call, my stress inflates like a hot air balloon.

I have to trust that I'm interpreting this correctly—that unless you give me peace, it's not the time to call. Waiting on you, Lord, waiting on you!

Back home, I turned the radio to the Christian station. Sermon broadcasts followed me around the house as I prepared for church.

A discussion of the relevance of Easter played in the background as I poured my coffee, pulled a chair up to the kitchen table, and wrote a little message to my husband of twenty-nine years. Having signed the card and propped it beside the one Rick had addressed to me, I popped some bread in the toaster and leaned on the counter, enjoying the aroma as the toast browned.

Lord, Rick has been at my side through so much. I wonder if either of us would have set foot down that aisle to happily ever after if we'd had an inkling of what was to come—job lay-offs, unemployment, the death of a baby, our son's diagnosis of Tourette Syndrome, bankruptcy, our daughter's accident and disability. Rick's been my rock.

We didn't start walking closely with you until a decade into our marriage. Some might think the troubles would have stopped when we made you the focus of our lives, but that wasn't the case. In fact, they intensified for quite a while. There was a difference, though. We were no longer alone in the struggle. It was in the midst of the chaos that we were able to see your hand here, there and everywhere.

If things had suddenly become easy, I might have attributed it to my own strength, not yours. We needed to see the contrast between crisis without Jesus and crisis with Jesus to truly grasp who you are in our lives

Looking back, I can see how much both of us have grown and matured since we decided to cast our lot with you. We have a long way to go, but we've definitely made progress. You were so right in your choice of a husband for me. I thank you with all my heart for drawing us together.

I set buttered toast and a banana beside my laptop and checked for morning emails. There was one new message in my inbox.

SUBJECT: Food?

Hey parents.
Can one of you give me dinner tonight? Matt's going biking with his buds and might not be back in time.
Draya

I wrote back:

Hey daughter.

Yes, we will feed you. Starving daughters do not make parents look good. Do you want to wheel on over here? The weather's supposed to be nice and it's only two blocks. Dad's planning to barbecue.

Mom

I hit "Send" then opened Facebook. At the top of my feed was a newly posted photo of Lawrence doting on his granddaughter, Josie. Lawrence was spending Easter weekend in Calgary visiting his son, Shaemus, and family. Shaemus had added a comment under the photo: "Poppa comes to visit Josie. Not sure if he remembers she has parents! LOL"

I noticed a message alert and clicked on the icon. It was from Shaemus. "Hi Auntie Bobbi. Dad's saving roaming charges on his cell phone. He says he talked to Grandma and you should call her and offer to take her for groceries. She's ready now."

Call Grandma. Like a heavy shroud, a weight settled on my heart. Without warning, tears began to well. I sighed and reached for a tissue.

Jesus, I didn't realize I was still this upset about that last encounter with Mom. The idea of purposefully walking into a situation where she may or may not explode feels enormous.

Mentally, I stepped back. What was I feeling?

I needed to let this simmer for a bit, and the shower is a good place to release any tears we'd rather not acknowledge.

A radio program had begun by the time I came back to the kitchen, wrapped in my old navy robe. On my way to pour a second cup of coffee, I caught a sentence in the message being broadcast: "You don't do something because you feel like it. You do it because you're anointed to do it!"

My mouth dropped open and I stopped in my tracks. I couldn't help but shake my head in amazement. *Lord, you do get it. I don't know if anyone else realizes how much of a battle I have to fight when it comes to being Mom's support, but you do, don't you?*

Thank you for caring so much that you would orchestrate this radio message on my behalf. You are so gentle, so kind. And so persistent! Yes, Lord, I'm listening.

The broadcast continued. The pastor was contrasting two of Jesus' disciples, Peter and John. Peter was always telling Jesus, "I love you, Lord!" Peter was impulsive, jumping in, trying to make things happen. He did right things, but he also made mistakes. John on the other hand called himself "the disciple Jesus loved." He didn't seem to feel pressured to take action. Instead he went with the flow.

You were John's flow, Jesus. Is that what I'm supposed to understand? I'm making a big deal out of being obedient, as though you won't love me if I don't do the right thing. But maybe that's not the real issue. You love me—plain and simple. It's not about what I do or how well I do it. It's about the fact that you love me, no matter what.

So, if I call Mom, that's good. That's what I understand I should do. But I've made this into works, and that's wrong. If I don't call, it won't change how you feel about me.

Something else just occurred to me. Mom's response doesn't change how you feel about me, either. Oh my! That's so important! If she blasts me again, you still love me. Her action towards me doesn't diminish me in your eyes.

I have to remember that you are Lord over Mom's life. I can't control what she does, how she reacts. If our conversation goes sideways, you promise to still be responsible for her.

If she makes accusations again, I can politely say goodbye, leave her with you, and carry on.

Nine-thirty. Call now? Sure! But I am not doing it to make myself feel good. Or to make myself worthy of your love. I am doing it because I want to feed your sheep.

I felt so full of the Lord's anointing, it was easy to pick up the phone and dial.

"Happy Easter!" Mom answered cheerfully after the fourth ring.

"Happy Easter to you too! It's Bobbi. How are you doing?"

"It really is warm. There are still so many puddles. I haven't gone out."

No mention of the other call and no mention of her accusations; we chatted for a few minutes about the weather, and the coming spring.

"I was going to call you today," Mom said suddenly. "I need your help. I got a phone call. Well, no. I think it was a letter. I don't have… yes, a call. My taxes. I sent in my taxes. The accountant? His name is Solbey. And his girl. Do you know them?

"No, I don't."

"But they have more papers that have to be signed. Maybe I did it wrong. I hope not. The government, you know. There could be trouble. I'm scared. I'm really scared. I mailed them. Mailed them in on time."

"You always do your taxes carefully, Mom."

"Well, not this time. I thought I'd be dead by now, so I didn't keep my records very well."

"You thought…you thought you'd be dead?"

"Well yes. I am eighty. I think. Am I eighty now?"

"You're ninety, Mom.

"Really? Am I? In any case, I thought I'd be dead, and then you could worry about it. So it took me weeks and weeks to do them."

I gulped, not knowing whether to laugh or be annoyed. Diplomatically, I did neither.

"If there's a problem, I'm sure it's just something little. I have tomorrow off for Easter Monday. I expect your accountant will be open. How about I come and get you around eleven? We can get your papers signed and then go for lunch. Would that work?"

"Oh, yes. I thought I'd have to take a cab. I wasn't sure of the number. You'll come tomorrow? What time?"

"Around eleven. Do you want me to call before I leave?"

"Well, no, of course not. I'll write it down. I can remember. I'll have my taxes ready. I've been going through the years, finding it all. So many boxes. How are you supposed to know? What do they want? She said investments. And I think T4s? Do you know about that?"

"I'll come early enough that we can sort through your papers and take what you might need. Okay?"

"That would be lovely. What time will you come? I should write it down."

"Eleven. I'll come around eleven."

"What would I do without you?"

"Well, you don't have to worry about that because you have me," I said magnanimously. "I'll see you tomorrow. Have a lovely Easter."

"You, too. Bye-bye."

"Bye-bye."

So simple. You knew she needed help, Lord, and you brought me around to a place where I could feel okay about calling her. Tomorrow we'll get the accountant taken care of, have lunch, maybe get groceries...

I paused to check my heart.

Hmmm...nope. No resentment...and I will refuse to think that I'm losing my holiday Monday, because all the days are your days.

I have to admit, though, this fight against the natural self is a real pain. Sometimes I feel as if I'm living Paul's description of his inner battle in Romans chapter seven. At least I know I'm in good company. Thank you, Lord.

Chapter Nineteen

*T*o be safe, I called Mom before leaving the next morning.

"Are we still going to the accountant's?" I asked after we'd exchanged hellos.

"Will you drive me?" Her voice trembled a little. "I think they said they changed offices. I don't know if I can find it on the bus."

"Yes, I'm going to drive you. I'll be there in half an hour. Do you have the new address?"

"I'll find it," she said in a stronger voice.

"See you soon, then."

As I drove, doubt set in.

Lord, has Mom really forgotten her accusations that Lawrence and I were stealing from her, allegations voiced so firmly only a couple of weeks ago? Is her friendly response simply because she needs help, and I'm the only one available to provide it?

Jesus quickly reined in my thoughts.

I guess it's irrelevant, isn't it, Lord? I'm going to go and help in any case. No sense in wasting time pondering what doesn't matter. Instead, please make me a blessing. And help me understand when she's trying to communicate.

The day was sunny and Mom had left the main door ajar. Coming up the steps, I could hear her radio blaring at top volume through the screen. The all-talk station seemed to be her constant companion these days.

Mom saw me through the window and came to greet me. "I'm so glad you came. I don't know how we're going to do this. They make it impossible!" She indicated the Yellow Pages, opened to the section marked Accounting Services. "I've been looking and looking," she fretted, "but the print is too small. I can't find it. I can't."

"What's the name of the company?"

"Soley? Stoney? Oh, I don't know," she fumed, smacking the offending yellow newsprint.

"Is that their envelope?" I queried, indicating a fat brown package in Mom's hand. She looked at it in surprise.

"What is this?" She handed it to me.

On the corner was the name of the firm, Solbey & Co. and an address. I had no way of knowing how old the envelope was, so to be safe, I dialed 411.

"It's a good thing we called," I told her after hanging up. "We would have gone to the wrong place."

"Why do they make it so hard," she objected. "I should be able to find an address. Stupid. I'm so stupid!"

It felt as though any words of encouragement might stir up more anxiety, so on that note of despair, we headed out, correct address and brown envelope in hand.

The office tower was new, sleek, and modern—so modern, in fact, that neither of us could find a directory on the wall. And why would we? In days gone by, companies moved into an office building and remained there for decades. Today, businesses come and go, change locations, change floors, change cities. A permanent directory would be a waste of money. Still, something must have taken its place.

Standing in the large, vacant lobby, Mom and I turned north, then west, then south and finally east. All we saw were elevators and the fire exit door. I began another circuit, more slowly this time, studying every surface. There had to be something.

Then I saw it. Embedded in a wide, tiled pillar in the centre of the lobby was a touchscreen monitor. Scrolling across the pale blue background the words "Centre Directory" danced and swooped, drawing attention to their happy mission.

"Here we go, Mom," I said, relieved. "I think this is what we're looking for."

"What is that? A TV? Why do we want a TV?"

"It says it's the directory. Let's see if we can figure it out."

I use computers daily, but I was unfamiliar with this kind of touchscreen technology. I attempted to appear confident as I tried to navigate my way through the program. Annoyance quickly set in.

User-friendly, my foot. Why don't they have steps one, two and three instead of making me poke randomly all over the screen?

After several unnecessary taps, the screen began to yield enough information that I was able to get a sense of the process. I worked to contain my frustration.

It won't help either of us if I get grumpy, Lord. Help, please!

Believing I'd figured out the next step, and hoping it would make Mom feel a little more in control, I tried to involve her.

"See here? There are two options: *Commercial* and *Individuals*. If I touch the word *Commercial* we should see all the companies."

I tapped the word and a list of several businesses appeared.

"Solbey & Company should be right...hmmm. It's not here."

Mom's silence was tangible. I glanced at her just as her rheumy eyes turned from the screen and looked at me.

I wonder what's going through your mind? I don't want to tell you what I'm thinking. I'm feeling as inept as you feel right now.

I smiled sheepishly and took a deep breath. "Well, then. Let's try the other option. We have to get out of this window."

Mom's eyes turned back to the screen, then to the wall of glass looking out onto the street.

"Window?" she said, incredulously. "Don't we go out the door?"

"No. Not those windows. The program window. Well, it's not really a window. It's just what they call it because you see something different in each one."

Mom looked at the monitor again, then back to me, staring blankly.

Lord. Help me!

I searched the screen, and realized I was squinting.

The colors are engaging, but the contrast is weak. It sure makes it hard to read. Back. Back. Somewhere it has to say Back.

Eventually I found *Return* in the bottom right-hand corner.

Return? It's supposed to say Back. Deep breath. I can do this.

"Here Mom. Give it a try. Just touch this word right here. Yes. Where it says *Return*."

Perhaps this will pique her interest and help both of us feel a little more competent.

Mom tentatively reached an arthritic finger forward and suddenly jabbed the word as though she were poking someone's eye out. I could empathize.

The screen changed again. Now we could access the second list through its title, *Individuals*.

"Here, Mom. We'll try this category. You just need to touch this word now."

With each progressive step, Mom was more reluctant. Doggedly, I guided her hand. Her finger managed to bump the next icon before she pulled away from me. Taking a step back, she clutched her envelope all the tighter. This, at least, was something tangible she could understand.

I breathed a sigh of relief when I saw Solbey & Co. in the list that appeared.

"We did it, Mom. See? Here's the room number. Tenth floor. We know where to go now."

Mom showed no indication that she shared my elation. Turning slowly, she followed me to the elevator. I pushed the call button and we waited in the elegant lobby, feeling like two fish out of water.

Lord, Mom retired long before home computers were invented. She's never lived in a house with a desktop or laptop. She doesn't watch TV anymore. For her, touchscreen technology must be akin to science fiction.

If this little exercise is leaving me feeling out of touch, what must it feel like for Mom and all those in her generation?

As we entered the elevator, Mom stepped back from the panel, relinquishing even this small task.

I pushed the tenth floor button and we rode up in silence.

Small, ornate letters on a brass plate directed us to Solbey & Co. I pulled on the heavy wooden door. *Mom would never have managed to open this herself.*

The office smelled of leather and oozed sophistication. I glanced at my jeans and Mom's faded jacket, two sizes too big now that she was so frail.

We were greeted warmly. "Hello. Welcome to Solbey & Company. I'm Dorothy. How can I help you?"

Silently Mom laid her huge envelope of papers on the counter.

"This is Nancy Bastion," I said when it became clear Mom wasn't going to offer anything more. Dorothy looked at Mom kindly, with raised eyebrows and a rueful smile.

"Oh no, Mrs. Bastion. We don't need any additional documentation. Didn't I say that on the phone? You only have to sign one document. You sent in a T4A after we completed your claim. We had to change it, so we need another signature to acknowledge that."

A simple legal requirement on the accountant's part, but by now the exercise bordered on the ridiculous. Mom had no understanding of what she was signing and why. Still, she had to jump through this hoop so the accountants could do their job.

Together, Dorothy and I pointed to the line marked with an 'X.'

Mom glanced at her envelope as though it might help clear her confusion. Her blue-veined hand tried to grip the sleek, silver pen proffered by the receptionist, but fumbled. She picked it up again and peered at the paper.

"Right here. By the 'X,'" Dorothy encouraged.

The 'X' had been written with a yellow highlighter. I wondered if Mom's eyes could see it against the white paper. I pulled my hand away, letting Dorothy take the lead.

Mom continued to hesitate, floating the pen in the vicinity of the receptionist's pointing finger. The pen began to lower. Closer. Closer.

"Here?" she said tremulously.

"Yes!" Dorothy and I said in unison.

Trying to replicate the beautiful script she had always taken such pride in, Mom carefully inscribed her name. The letters of *Nancy E. Bastion* trembled and sloped down below the line as she completed the task.

She looked at it with dismay. "I did it wrong. I'm sorry," she said, her voice quaking.

"No problem," Dorothy said, brightly. "Your name is all we need."

"Thank you." Mom's voice was unsteady as she turned away.

"Here are your papers," Dorothy called out.

I turned and retrieved the heavy envelope and we took our leave.

As we made our way down the hall, Mom suddenly found her voice again. "Is it reasonable to expect someone to ride the bus to this place just to provide one signature? What are they thinking?"

I didn't try to explain all that went through my mind.

Most people have other options. They can still drive. They can fax or scan the signed document and send it electronically. They can call and request it be mailed out, and then mail it back. They can even switch to an accountant closer to home. But for Mom and others in her generation, the old way is the only way. And it's fast disappearing.

Back in the car, Mom slumped in her seat, appearing defeated. "I never would have found this on my own," she muttered.

"Then it's a good thing we can do it together," I said, trying to offer encouragement. But I knew she was right.

Lord, what's going to happen to this generation of seniors? In a world where technology is rolling forward with the unrelenting power of a tsunami, Mom and thousands like her are being left behind in the debris of outdated systems and obsolete equipment.

I have to wonder. How long will it be before I too am left behind.

Meals and Money

Closed Bible on my lap, empty teacup beside me, I rocked back and forth in my comfy chair, gazing out the living room window. *What a lovely sunny Saturday. Lord, Mom and I haven't had a relaxing visit for ages. Every time we meet, something stressful happens. Maybe I should just take her out for a good time. No agenda, nothing to take care of, just time together. What do you think?*

I paused.

Peace.

Thank you, Lord. That's what we'll do then.

Mom was pleased to be invited for lunch. "Can you stop at the optometrist for me? They called and said my glasses are ready. They're $169. I have the money here."

"I sure can," I told her, relieved to be able to carry out the task on my own. Navigating the length of the mall left Mom too tired for anything else. Counting out her money in the privacy of her kitchen would be easier as well.

I recalled a conversation with Lawrence after his last visit.

"You know how she's been saying the bank won't let her withdraw her money?" he had said.

"She's been complaining about that for a while," I agreed

"Well, I went to the bank with her, and she was right. They asked for photo ID and when she couldn't produce it, the teller tried to turn her away. I went straight to the manager. I told him that Mom had banked at her local branch for thirty-five years, and everyone there knew her. No ID was necessary. I said it was the bank that had closed her branch and moved her account to this big, anonymous location. I told him it was his job to figure out how this loyal customer could access her accounts. Then, I just stood there, waiting."

"Bravo!" I cheered. Lawrence has always been more confrontational than I have. It was a blessing to tagteam with him in things like this. "So, did he find a solution?"

"He did. They made Mom an access card. It's like a debit card, but it doesn't work at the ATM, only at the teller. I used my name as the password so she can remember it. Now when she goes to the bank, she just has to pull out this card and she can get her money."

Lawrence was obviously pleased with his success and so was I. I hoped Mom was as well.

Mom was dressed and ready for our outing when I arrived. Swiss Chalet was the restaurant of choice, and we headed off. She tried on the new glasses before we pulled away from the curb, pronouncing them, "Wonderful. Absolutely wonderful!"

A great start to our visit, Lord. May it stay this way!

I'd planned our arrival for a half hour before the lunch rush on purpose. With no lineup, the hostess greeted us immediately. "This way, please."

Settled into a booth, we perused the lunch selections.

"Anything look good," I asked.

"I don't know. I can't read it very well. Why don't they turn on the lights?"

"It would help if they had brighter bulbs, wouldn't it. Let me read it for you."

I angled the menu towards the window, but the light created a glare on the laminated surface. Even I was squinting a bit.

The lunch special looked to be the simplest, so we ordered two quarter-chicken plates, and waited for our coffee to arrive. Mom chatted amiably, and I concentrated on her scattered conversation, working to decipher what she was trying to say. I felt like a student attending a lecture that was beyond my knowledge base. Chatting with Mom is not a relaxing pastime.

Oh, Mom. I wish I could make this easier for you. Your eyes can't read the menu. You don't hear half of what's said, and what you do hear gets garbled because of the dementia. No wonder you want to stay safe in your house where you know how to do things, where you can feel competent and capable.

The conversation had fizzled out. I don't do well with silence so I searched for a new topic.

"Did I tell you that I might be moving to a new office at work? The company is planning to expand."

"Do you have to build it?" Mom asked.

"Oh no," I explained. "They'll have contractors come in to do that."

"Well, someone has to do it. The airport will be sold and they'll build too. Are you going to invest?"

I quickly searched my brain for anything related to the airport. Ah, yes. I recalled a recent news story that Mom must have heard on the radio. "I did hear the city's planning to redevelop that land," I commented. "I don't know what they plan to do with it."

"All the children need to. It's just money. If they don't now they never will."

"I expect you're right."

I wonder what she's getting at? Does she want the family to invest in the airport land? Does she want to give some of her money to the family so they can invest it? Maybe I should attempt to clarify but I don't want to get Mom upset. I just want us to have a relaxing time together. Agreement is the plan, at least for today.

Our order arrived and I willingly put conversation aside to focus on eating. Mom's ability to use utensils seemed to have deteriorated. I watched as she attempted to stab her chicken with a spoon, then pushed a carrot off the plate in an attempt to secure some mashed potato. The server freshened her coffee. Mom's hand patted the basket holding creamers and sugar packets. She selected a few different creamers before settling on one. Her blue-tinged fingertips picked at the foil lid. I held back from taking it and opening the creamer for her. I knew such help would not be welcome. Painfully, I watched as she lifted a portion of the lid and turned the creamer over. Then, perhaps because it had taken so long and she no longer remembered the goal of the task, Mom carefully poured cream on her vegetables. I said nothing as she picked up her spoon and fork and tackled the chicken breast on her plate. Quietly I reached for another creamer and added it to her coffee, sliding the cup a little closer to her hand.

Suddenly she spoke up. "There ought to be a place where you can get a meal. Nearby. Where you don't have to walk too far. Just a couple of times a week." I hadn't noted it earlier, but now I realized that Mom had attacked her chicken dinner with great zeal.

Is she eating regularly? Is she eating proper meals? Watching her try to manipulate the utensils, it's almost as though she's out of practice. I need to pay more attention to what she buys when we shop for groceries.

"There's a little café over by the old bank, Mom. You know, where your dentist used to be. What if you were to go there for dinner sometimes? It's just a couple of blocks…"

"Oh no! It's a dive. You don't know if they even clean the dishes. You can't eat in places like that!"

Okay. No café. What about Meals on Wheels? Hmm…thinking back to the home care fiasco, would she even let the person in?

What about frozen dinners? She's never used a microwave, and the oven hasn't been repaired since she burned those cookies. Lord, I'm open to suggestions. I have no idea what to do, what Mom might allow. I'm turning this one over to you.

I quietly set out my credit card, hoping that I could pay for the meal and not have to make Mom struggle with the financial part. Mom noticed the card.

"Do you know what your brother did? I can't believe him sometimes. I just can't believe him."

"What did Lawrence do?"

"I went to the bank. He was here so of course he had to push in on it. He can't just let me do things alone."

I resisted the urge to smile.

Mom's perspective always seems skewed from ours. Lawrence and I will keep trying to help, but we must never make appreciation the criteria.

Mom continued with her version of the story. "I went to the bank and Lawrence came with me. All of a sudden there he is, talking to them about my money. My money! And once he opened his mouth, they talked to him from then on. Not to the old lady standing there. Like I was nothing!"

Once again I marvelled at the fact that when Mom's blood is pumping, her articulation improves dramatically.

"They didn't talk to me at all! But it's my money", she huffed. "I'm the one with money in their bank. They shouldn't be able to talk to him about my money. And this card. It's Lawrence's card. It lives in my purse but it's his card. So now is it his money?"

Lawrence's card? Oh! Of course. He made his name the password so she'd be able to remember it. Well, it's working. She remembers.

I listened and nodded, focusing on my goal that today would be one of agreement and nothing else. Besides, listening seemed more important than arguing or explaining.

By the time Mom's tale was concluded, the server had completed the transaction and our bill was paid. I helped Mom into her coat, and we went to the car.

Gusts of wind threatened to topple Mom in the parking lot. I held her arm as I unlocked the car with my remote. Once inside, Mom pulled an envelope from her purse. In it was cash, ready to reimburse me for her glasses.

"You count it out now. I counted it before we left. You count it to be sure."

Oh, no. She's watching me like a hawk, and counting along with me. There's no way I can hide the fact that it's $54 short. If I was alone, I'd willingly take the shortfall to save her the embarrassment.

"$115. There's $115 here, Mom."

"I can't believe it," she stammered. "I counted that again and again and again. How could it still be wrong?"

"The bills tend to stick together sometimes. I bet that's what happened." I tried to placate her without being patronizing, but she remained bleak.

"Stupid. Just stupid. A stupid old lady."

"Do you want to get a few groceries?" I queried, trying to change the subject.

"I guess you must," she said with a defeated tone.

Silently we left the parking lot and headed down the road.

At Safeway Mom struggled to release the seatbelt in the car. I waited quietly, allowing time for her to manage a task she'd done a thousand of times, a task that now, in her despondent state, was almost beyond her. When she finally climbed out of the seat she glared at the car as she spoke to me.

"You're so patient," she said, her voice tinged with bitterness. It didn't feel like a compliment.

This has to be so exasperating for you, Mom. I can navigate these simple tasks with ease, but for you, they get more difficult as the weeks go by. You're trying so hard to force your brain to work, to find ways around the gaps that keep opening. Even so, I get the sense that you're starting to admit this is a losing battle. I can't imagine what it must feel like for you, and I don't know how to make it easier.

She didn't ask me to let her practise using the quarter to release a shopping cart. She'd always insisted I talk her through it, "in case I have to do it on my own one day." The repetition hadn't helped. Her brain couldn't grasp the mechanical connection between inserting the coin and pushing out the key and chain. She wasn't able to create this new memory. Each time we practised, she was starting from scratch. I was both relieved and concerned when today she stood back and let me do it myself.

It's not me she's angry with, Lord. Of that I'm sure. It's one thing for Mom to struggle in private, but when we go out together, she has to struggle in front of me. For someone so fiercely proud and independent, I expect shame is a large part of her anger

I watched closely as Mom filled her shopping cart. None of the choices required cooking, or any real preparation. There were few canned goods. I recalled Mom saying how hard it was for her to work a can opener now. Her hands aren't strong enough. Some time ago I had found an electric opener that sits on top of the can and goes around by itself. If you don't wiggle it on exactly right, though, it won't start. I could see that as a result, canned soups and stews were no longer an option.

As we stood in line at the checkout, I did a quick inventory.

It looks like Mom's diet consists of eggs, cheese, yogurt, tea and canned milk, bread and jam, and bananas. Even cookies are a challenge because so often they're hard and hurt her teeth. But we did get her favourite Dairy Milk chocolate bar. So far, chocolate hasn't betrayed her!

Mom dug deep into her purse and pulled out an envelope. There in the checkout line she flared and counted four hundred dollars made up of fifties and twenties. Surreptitiously I scanned our fellow shoppers. Was anyone taking undue notice?

Resigned to allowing Mom control over her affairs, I offered a quick prayer.

Lord, one more task for you. Please protect us as we go to the car and drive home. Don't let any muggers see us or follow us.

When we arrived back at her house I helped Mom carry the groceries into the entryway. Halfheartedly she invited me in for tea. I begged off. I sensed that Mom wanted to be alone, perhaps to grieve the loss of her competency in a world crumbling under her feet like an eroding cliff.

∽⋙⋘∽

Driving home, I felt some of the grief and hopelessness Mom seemed to be expressing.

Our trip to the accountant with its computer monitor for a directory, dealing with business transactions by fax and email, bank access cards, even coin-connected shopping carts are the kinds of tasks that are beyond many in Mom's generation.

A senior senior, she calls herself.

Technology and increased security, all dressed up shiny and slick, adorned with bells and whistles, apps and icons, is developing faster than anyone seems able to keep up with. It seems to be assumed that this is what everyone desires. Isaiah's comment came to mind: "As for an idol, a metalworker casts it, and a goldsmith overlays it with gold and fashions silver chains for it" (Isaiah 40:19).

Lord Jesus, this is such a difficult time of transition. For Mom's generation, and many in mine as well, it doesn't feel like technology is something to embrace. Instead, it feels like the high-tech world is like a rat leaving a sinking ship. The ship is Today, and Today is no longer desirable. Everything around us says, "Leave the old ways behind." Tomorrow has become the place to be—tomorrow, where technology is the gold and silver god everyone seeks, the one to which everyone bows down.

But there's a generation of seniors left in the hold of that ship. There's a generation of baby boomers who are finding it harder and harder to scramble into the lifeboats.

Lord, you devised our brains so we could discover these technologies. As creator of creation, you already know where we're going to go as we keep inventing and progressing. I can have hope, because I know this life is temporary—a learning ground for our next life with you.

Those of us who know you can be assured that you're still in control. As long as we stay close to you, you'll watch over us as technology whooshes on by.

But what of those who don't know you? Those who think this life is all there is—one in which they're obsolete and being discarded along with rotary telephones and TV antennas. For them, Lord, I pray. May they come to know your truth and the hope that comes with it.

Changing Lightbulbs

*T*he sun shone through the car window. It was a little higher in the sky now that spring was encroaching on our long Alberta winter. Rick wound our Ford sedan through the residential streets of Mom's neighbourhood.

"She sounded so good on the phone," I told Rick. "Now that the weather is warmer and the sidewalks are bare, she's walking outside every day. I think the exercise and sunshine are helping. She probably has a better appetite as well."

"Sleeping better too," Rick agreed as we pulled in front of her house.

"I'll make some tea while you change her lightbulbs," I told him. "She said there were three or four that need replacing."

"Consider it done."

I knocked. Nothing. *Is the radio on?* I knocked again, a little harder this time. Still nothing.

I counted thirty seconds, as was my habit. This time I pounded. After a moment, the deadbolt turned in the lock. Cautiously, Mom opened the door. The radio blared a financial talk show in the background, as usual not quite fully tuned in.

"Oh. Hello. When did you come?"

Hesitantly Mom opened the door a bit wider and ushered us into the entry. She seemed to be searching for a reason for our presence.

"I'm not quite ready," she stammered before I could help her remember why we'd come. Quickly she went to the phone and touched the notepad, then to the kitchen counter to move the kettle over.

I've seen this stalling tactic before. It's as though she understands she should know why we're here but can't find the information readily available in her mind. I bet she's going to start offering everyday phrases to fill the space until she can figure out what's going on.

"Have you had a nice day?" she asked, pushing papers around on the kitchen table.

"We have," I replied.

"Busy, busy. Just so many things, aren't there?"

"There are indeed."

"There's a list, I'm sure," she muttered as she searched the papers on her table. "Groceries cost so much." She picked up her purse and peered inside, pulling out her wallet. "This is here," she explained as she glanced up. "You can't be sure, though."

As she made eye contact, I took advantage of the brief connection. "Did you still want Rick to replace your lightbulbs?" It took a moment before the subject found its home.

"Oh, yes. Can you do that? It's so dark in here."

Leading us into the spare room, Mom drew Rick's attention to the burned out overhead fixture, but I was noting something else. The spare bed and floor were covered with open files and shoeboxes. Numerous collections of envelopes were stacked in precarious piles—envelopes containing old bills, envelopes within envelopes, envelopes gathered into bundles tied with string, others tucked together in plastic bags along with scribbled notes and yellowed newspaper clippings. Elastics and paperclips strained to hold the bundles together in a semblance of order.

"You've been sorting your papers?" I commented.

"Oh. Oh. I hate this. I hate it. I was trying to sort them by year. You have to do that. But the Visa was here and the cards. And I had the car repairs. I think you have to tell the government about that. So I pulled those out. And I found the doctor bills from when your brother was sick. I couldn't find the one when you broke your leg. But look at this," she encompassed the chaos with a wave of her arm. "Look at it. What if Revenue Canada calls?"

"You just finished up your taxes last month, remember? We went to Solbey's and signed the forms. You're all done for the year now."

I waited. Rick waited.

Mom looked at her wallet, still clutched in her hand, and blinked. Purposefully she set the wallet down and pulled a shoebox toward her, shuffling through the papers inside.

A moment later she whisked an old receipt book from the pile and turned, confronting Rick. She shook the pad, flapping the worn pages. "You take this. Or you can throw it out. It has to go somewhere."

On the front, in black marker, were the words, "Rent Receipts 1982." I recalled that 1982 was the year Rick and I rented my childhood home from Mom, back when we were first married. We lived there for three years before she sold it.

"Thanks, Nancy. I'll put it in my files at home." Tucking it in his shirt pocket, Rick patted it and nodded affirmation. Mom nodded back.

Lord, thank you that Rick is so adaptable in all this. No explanations needed, just acceptance. Help me be that easygoing.

Released from the receipt book, Mom now seemed able to move forward, but lightbulbs had once again fallen from her radar. "My cupboards are bare," she tried to joke, leading us back to the kitchen. "Isn't there a word?"

A word? My brain searched for a translation. *Oh. A list.*

I found a piece of paper and wrote a few items on it.

"Here's a start," I offered. "Eggs, cheese, some canned milk and bread. Can you think of anything else?"

She paused, a quizzical look crossing her face, shook her head and put the list in her purse. "Somewhere there are, you know. Foot coverings. The cold," she tried to explain.

"Here are your boots," Rick gestured to the tray by the door.

"Of course."

Mom sat and with some effort pulled them on. I noticed how hard it was for her to bend her knee enough to reach her foot.

She manages when I'm not here, though, so I'm going to hold back from helping.

"Do you want your heavy coat or is the light one okay?" I asked.

As Mom and I got ready to go out, Rick took advantage of the distraction. Quickly he replaced the bulbs in the bedroom and then in her living room lamp. Mom's blue-grey eyes blinked as they registered the brightened atmosphere. A warm smile showed her pleasure.

I expected we'd have tea and change the lightbulbs. Now it looks like we're going grocery shopping. Ah well. No matter. Adaptability. Right, Lord?

Together we made our way out to the car, Mom holding Rick's arm as they clambered over the frozen mud-caked remains of the winter drifts next to the curb. I opened her door and waited while she climbed in.

"Light is light," Mom declared as I pulled the seatbelt over her shoulder.

"It is that." I handed the buckle to Rick so he could insert it from the driver's side. Mom brushed a hand along the strap crossing her chest, trying to shove it away. She pushed her arm under the strap and nudged it over her head and behind her shoulder. I decided it wasn't worth an argument, and quietly slipped into the back seat.

"Did you have plans today?" she asked, turning to Rick.

"What did you have in mind?"

"Very often. Well. Lunch too. They always did, you know."

"Lunch it is," Rick agreed and started the car.

"Swiss Chalet?" I suggested from the back seat.

"What a lovely idea!" Mom sighed, turning her face to the sun.

It's like changing TV channels, Lord. In the course of an hour, Mom has gone from papers to visitors to groceries to lightbulbs to papers to receipt

books, and back to groceries again. She's dressed for the weather, recognized the improvement in lighting, and ultimately ended up in a restaurant.

Lord, my brain is exhausted! These rapid mental changes are hard for me. How much harder must they be for Mom.

If we're going to keep moving forward, plans must be fluid. Expectations have no place when a mind flickers in the grips of dementia. Help me remember that each day will be its own. One day, this day, is all you require of Mom and of me. "Therefore do not worry about tomorrow, for tomorrow will worry about itself. Each day has enough trouble of its own" (Matthew 6:24).

Trouble enough of its own? That certainly describes Mom's life these days. Mine too at times. I decided months ago that you were going to be my only resource as I try to help Mom navigate her life with dementia. So far, you've met every need. Thank you for your faithfulness.

Mother's Day Intruders

I frowned as yet another ad filled the screen, blotting out the morning news— "May 8th. Don't forget that special person in your life!"

I scratched Maggie's ears and lectured her as she stared at me with shiny marble-like eyes.

"Every year, calendars across North America proclaim Mother's Day. Honestly, Maggie. It drives me nuts. With it comes a flurry of expectations and obligations. The assumption is that every mother-child relationship is positive, but it's just not so."

Maggie adjusted her furry body so I'd have better access to her tummy. My grumblings didn't seem to be of much interest to her so I directed my comments to Jesus.

Lord, you created all sorts of celebrations and festivals for the Jewish nation. Every one of them focused on worshiping you, a God who never lets his children down. Today, like King Nebuchadnezzar of old, we create days to honour ourselves. Then we validate them by supporting greeting card companies, bakeries, restaurants, flower shops, gift shops, and a myriad of other industries, all to set a human being on a pedestal.

Worshipping God is never a letdown. Worshipping people is a very different story. Obligatory occasions like Mother's and Father's Day raise expectations that can cause a great deal of hurt when they're unfulfilled.

Today Facebook is covered with, "Share if you love your mother!" sentiments. I don't see anyone posting, "Share if you're struggling to survive your mother!"

I feel so discouraged. Scripture says we are to honour our father and mother. Will a Hallmark card cover it, or do I have to go and visit?

I'm a mother too, you know. Forgive my pouting, but today I'd rather spend a little time with my kids, and then have the afternoon to read and just hang out.

More scripture comes to mind:

For I was hungry and you gave me something to eat, I was thirsty and you gave me something to drink, I was a stranger and you invited me in, I needed clothes and you clothed me, I was sick and you looked after me, I was in prison and you came to visit me. *(Matthew 25:35-36)*

Needs. Mom has needs. I have needs as well, but you'll meet my needs in your way, in your time.

What I do for Mom, I do for you. Today I need to put aside my temptation to cater to myself and think of what you would want for her. You'd reach out your hand to one who is lonely and struggling. If I'm Jesus-in-skin for Mom, then that's what I'll be. I'll make the phone call with your love in my heart. The rest is up to you.

"Happy Mother's Day," I said brightly when Mom answered the phone.

"Hello! Your brother just called and said the same thing. I didn't know it was Mother's Day. What are you doing?"

"I'm calling to see if Rick and I can take you for lunch."

"Lunch? That would be lovely. And could we get groceries? My cupboards are bare. There's nothing to eat anymore."

"Lunch and groceries. Sounds like a plan."

"And Rick will come?"

"Yes, he will."

"He does such a good job of the sidewalks."

"He certainly does." I didn't mention that Mom had had a shovelling service over the winter, or that it was spring now and the snow was gone. I understood her point—that Rick is kind and helpful, an accurate observation.

I was grateful Rick was joining us. Mom always seems calm in his presence. I'd noted before that Mom compartmentalizes the few people in her life. In her mind, everyone has a role. Rick makes her feel safe and protected. Her behaviour around him reflects that.

Lawrence is the one she believes can be trusted with money and financial matters. He's also the one she dotes on and longs to see. Lately, though, when he's tried to help her understand by explaining her wrong interpretation of situations, she's been thrown into a tailspin. His interactions with her are not as positive as they used to be.

When Mom sees me, her brain seems to go directly to a list of tasks, whether they're needed or not. I'm her paid helper, since it's always her plan to give me that twenty dollars for my time and gas.

We purposely waited until two o'clock to pick Mom up. By then the Mother's Day rush would be done at the restaurant. Instead of a meal, we decided we would indulge in three different decadent desserts. Mom has an insatiable sweet tooth, so we divided each treat into three and shared the portions, giving everyone a taste sensation.

While we ate, Mom became serious. "You have to know about this. Someone does."

"Is something going on?" I asked.

"Who shouldn't? They always do and no one ought to. But they still do."

Lord, it's clear Mom has something important she needs to share. Please help us understand what it is.

"I can't just come out and make a cup of tea if I can't sleep. I miss that. It's not right."

"At night, you mean?" Mom always soothed herself with a cup of tea when she couldn't sleep. "Why can't you make tea at night?"

"Because they're out there."

"You mean there are neighbours making noise? By your house?"

"I used to get up and make tea. But now they're out there. I can't."

"In the neighbourhood?" I was having trouble getting a handle on the problem.

"Why would they be in the neighbourhood? It's dark out there."

"In your house, then? There are people in your house?" This was becoming disturbing.

"Of course. They're in the basement."

Lord, what's going on? What do I say?

"Do you see them in the daytime?" I asked.

"I hear them, but maybe they're outside then. Maybe they're next door. I don't know where they are."

"But at night you see them?"

"Of course I don't see them. I'm in my room."

She sounds calm, but annoyed. People in her house at night. This is bizarre.

"I keep my door closed," Mom continued, "so my light doesn't bother them. I have to put my housecoat on if I want to go to the bathroom."

She sounds like this is an inconvenience. Dare I explore a little further?

"Are you frightened of these people?" I asked. Mom looked a little perplexed at my question.

"No."

"But they're in your house."

"I hear them. I hear them at night. There are several. Different voices."

"What do they say?" I asked.

"Well, I can't really tell. They talk all the time, though."

I looked at Rick, but he just shook his head, eyebrows raised. It looked like I was on my own with this one.

People living in the basement, who talk a lot, and come up and use the house at night. Where in the world is this coming from? Lord, once again I'm at a loss. You're in charge. I give this to you.

We finished our desserts and stopped at Safeway, Mom's list in hand.

"I'll get a cart," I said, leaving Rick to help Mom out of the car.
"No. No! I need to learn how to do that. Rick can help me." She looked at him endearingly. "You can show me how, can't you? I know you're a good teacher."

I didn't take offence at her emphasis.

Lord, does Mom know she can't learn anymore? We've all been pretending for a long time that if we just try harder, if we find that magic strategy, she'll be able to maintain her independence. It's not going to happen, though, is it? The tasks she can no longer do are permanently gone and her tenuous ability to cope is going to deteriorate further.

I think Mom is aware of this, but I also think she wants to deny it for as long as she possibly can. It's a quandary. Do we try to force her to move out of her house, or just keep treading water? Lawrence and I have no legal power. I don't know what to do.

We filled a small basket with her usual fare. In the pharmacy section she picked up a bottle of aspirin and one of milk of magnesia, her only medications.

Back at Mom's place, Rick carried her groceries into the house. He and I received warm hugs as we said goodbye.

"Thank you for coming," Mom said, patting Rick's arm. "You're both such good kids. What would I do without you?"

"You're welcome, Nancy," Rick returned the pat, "and happy Mother's Day."

"We had a good time, Mom. I'll give you a call later in the week. Take care now."

I wish there was some way to bring Rick on every outing, Lord. Mom seems so much more relaxed when he's around. Too bad he works night shift. We did have a nice visit today, though. Thank you for that. But what about the spectre of nighttime intruders? What could that be about?

Security and a Dash of Hope

"*C*an Rick cut my grass?" Mom asked the moment she heard my voice on the phone.

"I'm sure he can, but isn't your lawn care service doing it?" G & D Landscaping had been managing Mom's yard work for years now, so her request surprised me.

"He didn't. This time his wife phoned. He's sick. Or broke something? I don't know. But now the grass is long. The city might come after me. I'm scared. I'm really scared."

"No need to worry," I told her. "Sunday should be sunny, and Rick's off work. He'll be happy to take care of it."

"Sunday? Oh, that would be wonderful. You don't think he'd mind?"

"Not at all. He told you before to let him know if anything needs doing. You can look for him this weekend."

"When will he come? I need to write it down."

"He'll come Sunday. Day after tomorrow."

"Is that Sunday?"

"Sunday. That's right."

Rick was willing to make his services available. Sunday he loaded the gas mower into the van and headed off to Mom's just after lunch.

I expected him back within the hour but dinner was almost ready when he came in the door.

I raised an eyebrow. He dropped his head.

"Food," he begged.

"Ten minutes."

"I'll clean up."

I dished out salad and chili, and joined Rick, ready to hear his tale.

"Well," he began after fortifying himself with a few bites. "I got started on the mowing and your mom came out and sat on the steps, watching me. She was smiling and talking, but of course I couldn't hear her. I finished the lawn in half an hour. There isn't much there. But then she said she had a couple of things to show me."

"Uh oh."

"Uh oh is right!"

He ate a few more bites, keeping me in suspense.

"So," he began again. "First she showed me inside the garage. She's cleaned it out really well, but her '78 Dodge is still sitting there. It's covered in dust, but in great shape. The body, anyway. I wonder if it runs."

"No idea. She parked it when the doctor wouldn't sign off on her driver's license. That was ten years ago."

"Beautiful chassis. Anyway, we poked around the garage, and then she gave me a tour of the yard…which I'd just toured with the lawnmower."

I chuckled. "You're so patient."

"I try." He nodded. "Then we went inside." He paused to dish himself some more chili from the pot on the stove. I waited, not hiding my impatience. I noted he was as bad as Lawrence as he savoured the moment.

"It seems she has a nightly routine," he said, making himself comfortable again. "She checks through the house to make sure everything is safe."

"That's good," I responded, but then noted his expression. "Isn't it?"

"Well, yes and no. Good to be safe, but perhaps she's a little obsessive."

"Uh oh," I said again.

"Uh oh is right."

After clearing our dishes, we moved to the living room. Rick hoisted the foot of his recliner and made himself comfortable before continuing.

"We started in the bathroom. She showed me how the taps have to be turned off, first the sink and then the tub."

"Probably from when she flooded the house last winter," I mused.

"Probably. But that was just the beginning. Next, she took me into the spare bedroom. First, she pointed out all her boxes of papers, and told me how everything important is in there, and if anything happened to her, that's where I'd find everything I needed. Then she opened the closet and showed me a few winter clothes hanging up. She waved her hands around and talked about the boxes and bags up on the shelf, and an old metal box in the corner, and a few cardboard boxes. She picked up a bunch of coat hangers and rattled those, going on and on. I really couldn't make sense out of what she was trying to say, so I just nodded."

"Wise."

"I thought so." He laughed. "But then she showed me that everything electrical was unplugged. The lamp. The little organ. The fan. I think she was making the point that if you leave things plugged in, they could start a fire."

"Well, I guess that's not such a big deal. She has the overhead light in there, so she can use the switch."

"My thought, too. But then we went into the living room. She showed me that the two standing lamps were unplugged. The only one working is the table lamp— the newer one, by the kitchen door."

"There's no overhead light in the living room."

"No, and that's a problem. She said at night it's very dark in there. She can't get around, and can't see to use the phone. I suggested she plug in the lamp by the phone table, but she got a little panicky, so I dropped it.

"The tour wasn't done, though. Next we went into the kitchen and she demonstrated turning the sink taps on and off. She turned the knobs on the stove burners on and off as well. She pointed out that the kettle and toaster oven were unplugged. I got the impression she doesn't feel safe using them anymore."

"She still uses the kettle for her tea," I interjected. "At least I hope she does!"

"There was a mug in the sink so I think so. Anyway, next we headed to the basement. Same routine down there.

"She showed me that the taps for the washer were turned off. We went into the suite and she did the same with the taps in the kitchenette and the bathroom. Taps are very important these days. She showed me the lamps and fan, all unplugged. She showed me the furnace and bent down to see that the flame was on. Then I had to bend down and look at it, too. She asked me, 'should this be on? Should that light be on?' So I explained it was the pilot light and that it stays on all the time, that the rest of the flame won't come on until it's cooler outside."

"Mom knows all that," I said. "She's maintained that furnace for forty years now. I'm sure she had the manual memorized within a month of having it installed."

"Not anymore. She seems to be afraid of it. She asked if she should put the fire out, but I explained the pilot light should always be lit unless the gas is turned off, otherwise she'll get gas in the house. That concerned her too, but I said it all looked good.

"While we walked around she was telling me random things that didn't make much sense. I couldn't really follow it, so I just nodded a lot."

"God bless your patient heart. You were gone four hours! You are a good son-in-law, hubby dear."

"I am," he said, laughing and picking up the remote. "I've earned a hockey game."

"You have, indeed."

⤬

Tuesday I stopped at Mom's after work. As usual, a radio talk show was blaring.

"Can we turn the radio down," I shouted as I followed Mom into the kitchen. She looked startled.

"Radio? Oh, yes. I don't even notice it," she said with a laugh, turning it off. "Do you want tea before we get groceries?" she asked.

I hoped we could talk about her afternoon with Rick, so I agreed. As Mom plugged the kettle in, I glanced at a few scraps of paper on the table. One of them looked to be a conversation starter.

Nancy's first checklist

Once the tea was ready, I picked up an envelope on which a list had been written. In red letters, it was entitled, "TO CHECK." Below were the items she'd shown Rick the Sunday before. This list numbered the order in which to check things:

1. Gas heater
2. Downstairs kitchen and sink, basement—dryer and washer, washcloths in sink
3. Hallway and toilet and shower, wash basin and toilet
4. Upstairs kitchen sink, bathtub, toilet

Also on the list was an additional reminder to check the upstairs sink, stove and toaster, and lock the upstairs back door.

"I see you have a checklist," I remarked casually.

"That one? That's the wrong one. That's old."

Mom got up and rushed into her bedroom. After a few moments she returned waving another piece of paper.

"Here it is. The right one. I did this with Rick. Rick knows all about it. He knows that everything is right now. If anything isn't he knows. He can take care of it."

The 'right' list

I looked over this second list. The items were similar, but less organized than the first.

"So you showed Rick around. Did he tell you everything looked all right?"

"He's such a smart man."

"He is," I agreed. "But did he say everything looked safe?"

"You have to be so careful. Anything could happen. This is an old house, you know."

"It is. But you've taken very good care of it. Rick told me he thinks you're doing a good job."

"I think we need groceries. Do you have time to get groceries?"

"Yes," I said brightly. "I have time for groceries. I've got my keys and my purse. How about you? Do you have your keys? Your shopping list?"

"Oh gosh. My list. I made a list. Where is it?" Looking in her purse, Mom saw a tattered paper and pulled it out. "Do you need this?" she asked.

"Let's see." I checked the three-year-old Visa statement. "No, I think that can stay here. Shall I put it on the table?"

"I paid that, I'm sure. Can you see if I paid it?"

"Yes, it's paid. It says so right here. Did you notice your grocery list in there?"

Digging a little deeper, Mom pulled out an envelope from a wad held together by a rubber band. This one was a request for a donation to a local charity.

"How many times do they ask?" she said petulantly.

"You get a lot of junk mail, don't you?"

"I wish they'd stop. I can't pay all of them. But see? That's my name. It says *Dear Nancy*. If I don't send them money, will they get mad?"

"It's just a mass mailing, Mom. They have computers now that add the name in there. It's looks personal, but it really isn't."

"How can you know? Who told you that?"

"They send me junk mail, too. These same people. I only send donations to a couple of places. The rest I throw away. No one's ever become upset with me. How about that grocery list? Do you see it in there?"

Rummaging some more, Mom pulled out a full page ad she'd taken from the *Edmonton Seniors* paper. In bold print, it announced they were taking applications for a new seniors' residence called Klassen Manor.

"Look at the people," she beamed.

Together we gazed at the picture of an elderly couple with larger-than-life denture smiles, dressed in expensive activewear outfits. They looked ready to pop off the page and do aerobics right there in the kitchen.

"Look how happy they are," Mom said wistfully.

I scanned the page. "Klassen Manor. It says it's new. In the west end. Is this a place you'd like to visit?"

Lord, ever since Mom made it clear our basement wasn't an option, I've given up hope for an alternative. Has Mom found a place where she thinks she'd be comfortable?

"I can't stay here forever. Someone has to. Just has to." She stroked the page and the smiling people. "Do you think they'd take me?" she asked.

"They'll take anyone who wants to pay their rent," I said and laughed. "Do you want me to give them a call and set up a visit?"

"Oh, no," Mom pulled back in alarm. "Don't do anything now. I don't want to jump into anything. You can't be too careful, you know. Maybe we can drive by. But don't talk to anyone. You never know what they'll make you do."

"We'll just keep it in mind, then. So, what about that grocery list?"

It took another fifteen minutes to find the list, Mom's keys and her shoes, stop to go to the bathroom, and have a quick discussion about the merits of university education versus the need for animal control. (I nodded and agreed with all her points.)

Grocery shopping was followed by the usual cinnamon bun and ice cream, and we hugged goodbye.

As I drove home, my mind drifted back to the advertisement that had so impressed my mother.

Klassen Manor. It's a twenty-five-minute drive, but if it's a place she thinks she'd like... Do I dare hope, Lord? I guess we'll wait and see. I can't believe Mom is actively thinking about making the move. How difficult it must be! After forty years in that house, the idea of leaving would be hard. I wonder how she'd manage in a new place. She has such difficulty carrying out her usual routines in a place she knows well. A strange apartment, different layout, a meal schedule, elevators...Lord, I pray you'll help Mom, and help me to assist her in making the right decision at the right time. I've tucked the name of the place into my head. Who knows what may come of this in the future?

Chapter Twenty-Four

JUNE

*L*awrence's oldest son, Shaemus, and his young family arrived from Calgary. They'd always enjoyed staying with us, but this time his wife, Joanne, was thrilled to try out the new bathroom, especially given the fact that they now had one-month-old Olivia as well as four-year-old Josie.

Lord, we never would have gone to the expense of adding a second bathroom if we hadn't thought Mom would live with us. Joanne's eyes lit up when she realized she wouldn't have to bring her little ones upstairs to use the washroom during their visit. *I still don't know why you got us going on the bathroom, but it's a welcome blessing for our guests, so thank you.*

Lawrence and his daughter, Sinead, were in town as well, staying with Mom.

Homemade burgers and a variety of salads were ready when Lawrence, Sinead and Mom arrived. The day was beautiful and we gathered in the back yard where Rick took the helm as cook.

Mom seemed happy and engaged, cuddling Olivia and watching Josie's antics.

At first, Mom listened and took part in the conversation. After a while, I realized her attention was elsewhere. She maintained a pleasant expression, but her eyes were focused past our group, almost as though she were mentally escaping the activity.

"Mom," Lawrence said when dinner was finished and cleared away. "We're going to have ice cream for dessert. Do you want chocolate or vanilla?"

I was filling bowls and Rick was serving as Lawrence made his offer.

"Oh, is it that time again? I don't really know who makes those decisions."

"What decisions are those?" Lawrence asked.

"I think it'll be on the news if you want to listen. We should listen for that."

I quickly stepped in.

"That's a good idea, Mom. We'll make sure we catch the news when it's time."

Without missing a beat, Rick slipped a bowl of ice cream into Lawrence's hand, and Lawrence smoothly shifted from choice to decision.

"Here's a spoon," he offered. "Rick's brought you some vanilla ice cream."

"Oh, thank you, Rick! How did you know I'd like that?" Mom tittered like a flirty teen.

"Just smart, I guess," Rick replied.

"Is anyone going to go for tomorrow?" Mom asked.

"I'm staying a few more days," Lawrence told her. "Then I'll go back home."

"How did you think of that? Who would tell you such things?"

"I guess we'll never know," Lawrence said ruefully.

Lord, following conversation with Mom is like trying to follow a butterfly. When several of us are present, the burden of conversation isn't on any one person, so it's easier for Lawrence and me. At the same time, I think it's harder for Mom. A group of people is too much for her to manage these days.

Nancy and son-in-law, Rick

JULY

Nancy and grandson, Luke

The plan was to go grocery shopping. I left work around two so I could be home by dinnertime. When Mom let me in, it became apparent the agenda had changed.

"Come in here. You need to know this," she said before I could put my purse down. I followed her into the spare room.

Opening each drawer in two old dressers, we inspected the contents. Carefully Mom showed me a broken gold watch and some old, discoloured jewelry. She also explained the workings of a chromatic harmonica I recognized from my childhood.

"These are silver coins," she explained as she unfolded a cloth napkin to display a worn bread bag containing a number of coins. Through the plastic I could see numerous notes, each saying the same thing: "A magnet will not pick up silver coins."

"The old coins have silver in them," Mom explained. "You need to keep them. They are valuable."

The coins, with multiple notes saying the same thing

Next to be considered was an envelope containing information about the Memorial Society. "This is who you contact...when I'm dead...they know."

"Okay."

I turned the afternoon over to Mom and switched my focus from groceries to estate planning. Clearly, this had been on her mind, and she would feel better if she could share what she needed me to know.

We spent the next few hours going through papers—shoeboxes and file boxes in the spare room, followed by two fire-proof locked boxes, one toolbox with a tiny padlock, and several more shoeboxes in her bedroom. Mom's filing system had always consisted of labelling the envelope in which a bill had come and storing each year's correspondence in a separate box. This had worked well for decades. Notations on older envelopes were clear and concise. There was a distinct change in notations made during the last few years, however.

"VISA bill. KEEP THIS. December 2009. REFERENCE."

"GIC INFORMATION. DO NOT THROW AWAY."

"EPCOR. Paid Sept 2010. $142.34. Cheque # 92. Cheque #. KEEP"

The contents of envelopes from the last year didn't always match the notations. Some envelopes were empty. Some contained a mixture of statements, newspaper articles, stain removal information and scraps of paper with notes Mom had written to herself. Carefully, Mom reviewed each item with me.

Two hours after my arrival, Mom plopped down on the side of her bed, looking exhausted. "I do this. I keep doing this. Hour after hour I go through these papers. I can't stop myself! I hate it but I can't stop! How do I stop?"

"We've covered a lot, Mom, and I think you've shown me everything I need to be aware of. Why don't I plug in the kettle and we can take a break?"

Tea and cookies seemed the key to helping break the loop of her obsessive-compulsive behaviour. I put the kettle on and found mugs in the cupboard. Mom didn't try to help. This was unusual. She sat quietly in her chair, watching me. As the minutes passed, she seemed to gain some distance from her papers.

"The radio people talk. Do you hear them?"

"The radio's not on right now, Mom," I said reasonably.

"Your brother says the people at night are from the radio. What does he know?"

Pieces fell into place.

"Do you leave your radio on all night, Mom?" Lawrence was the one who often slept over. He would know.

"What radio?"

"Your radio. Do you leave it on at night? If you do, that would be the voices you hear when you're in bed. It's not people from the basement. It's just the radio talk shows."

"Your brother says the same thing. Maybe that's right."

"I think it is," I smiled, relieved. Thank goodness that mystery had been solved.

"Did there have to be councillors for the city?" Mom changed the subject.

"You've been reading the news," I commented vaguely.

Mom rambled on as we enjoyed our snack. I nodded often, adding generic comments here and there.

"Have you been here?" Mom pulled a folded clipping from a pile of paper and lay it flat. The Klassen Manor advertisement was now a little tattered, but the denture-smiling seniors were unmistakable. Together we read through the information, exploring the details. I didn't try to push. We were both tired from an intense afternoon.

After tea, I gathered my purse and keys and headed home. It wasn't until I pulled into my driveway that I realized we'd never gone for groceries.

Lord, does she have enough food for another week? I sure hope so.

AUGUST

Sunday afternoon I phoned Mom just to touch base.

"The neighbours are calling the city. They'll come and give me a fine. I know it. I'm scared. I'm really scared."

"Why are they calling the city?" I asked.

"The yard. You can't have a yard like this! Someone has to do something!"

That afternoon Rick and I spent several very hot hours working our way through Mom's garden. A wild explosion of thistles and perennials had overrun what used to be a large vegetable garden. Mom hovered on the edge as we pulled what was dead and thinned what was alive. Occasionally Rick caught my eye. I don't think he'd expected so much physical labour when I'd invited him to join me for a visit.

By the time we left, the garden was presentable.

I hope Mom doesn't feel she still has to fret about it. It must be so hard to see things that need to be done and not have the ability to do it. She always took such pride in her garden and flowers. I wonder how I'll feel if I get to that state some day?

Nancy, Bobbi, and Draya enjoying lunch

September

Mom turned ninety-one today. After seeing her struggles to interact during our family get-together in June, I felt a big party would be too much for Mom to manage. Instead, Draya and I took her to Earl's Restaurant for a birthday lunch.

Mom is becoming less steady on her feet. Normally, I let her take my arm, and we manage well. Taking both Mom and Draya on an outing presented some challenges I hadn't anticipated. First, I positioned Mom where she could lean on the Draya's wheelchair-accessible van, but not get bumped by the ramp as I extended it from the side door, or by Draya's power chair as she wheeled into her front passenger position. It was touch-and-go for a moment as Mom tried to climb up the ramp before Draya made her way in. I pulled Mom back in time, and Draya wheeled forward, adjusting her chair until it locked into the bracket on the floor.

Next, I brought Mom up the ramp, helping her to duck so she wouldn't hit her head. Draya and I took up the front positions, so Mom was banished to the far back where one bench seat remained. The van has a lowered floor, allowing Draya to see out the front window. That sets the back bench ten inches higher than normal. I lowered a movable footrest and tried to help Mom step on it to get up to the seat, but it was dark in the back of the van and she was unable to see the step. I guided her foot by gently tugging on her pant leg, until she found the platform. Finally, she positioned her bottom on the edge of the bench seat and hip-walked her body back. Good for her! I set her feet on the footrest, then buckled her in.

As we drove, Mom made occasional comments. Draya answered as best she could. Despite being seated a distance from us, Mom seemed to enjoy looking out the window.

Arriving at Earl's meant going through the boarding procedure in reverse. Finally, we found our way into the restaurant. It was nice outside, and we accepted the server's invitation to take a table on the patio. Instead of having a meal each, we shared three different appetizers followed by a delicious dessert. Mom loved the food, but I think her greatest delight was in being with Draya. She takes such joy in her grandchildren.

Leaving the restaurant and dropping Mom off at home meant repeating the van procedure yet again. By the time I dropped Draya at her home, I was exhausted and ready for quiet time at my own patio table.

At times like this, Lord, I know what people mean by the "sandwich generation" of caregivers. One young, one elderly, and here I am, mashed in the middle, trying to meet the needs of both. One at a time is a challenge. Both at once? Perhaps a party would have been easier. Still, Mom and Draya enjoyed their time together, so it was worth it. Tiring, but worth it.

Chapter Twenty-Five

"Hey, Mom!" Draya acknowledged my entry as I let myself into her house. "Don't let the cats escape."

I quickly closed the door before their grey tabby Kingston managed to bolt. Aires, a sleek black and white creature who treated all visitors with disdain, glanced at me from his perch on the cat tree by the couch, sniffed and stared suspiciously until I broke our gaze.

I kicked off my shoes as Draya wheeled around the corner to join me.

"So where's Matt gone?" I asked.

"Peanut butter and banana sandwich, please." Draya gave me her lunch preference as I followed her into the kitchen. "He and the guys are biking in B.C., some place around Golden, I think. He should be back Sunday evening. Lizzie's coming from Calgary tomorrow to hang out, so you won't have to do all my meals."

"Well, that's no fun. It's the only chance I get to visit," I laughed. "Your wheelchair has never stunted your social life, that's for sure. Matt's the one who's a homebody. You and your girlfriends go partying, and he's here on the couch with his sports TV and iPad."

"'Tis true, 'tis true," she nodded sagely. "Unless he's biking. That gets him off the couch every time. How's Grandma doing?"

I popped some bread into the toaster and began cutting up a banana. "I think she's actually considering the idea of moving out of her house." As I prepared Draya's sandwich, shooing Kingston away from the tantalizing peanut butter scent, I described Mom's interest in the ad for Klassen Manor.

"Why don't we take her to visit?" Draya suggested.

"I don't know if she'd go for it. She got really anxious when I suggested setting up an appointment."

"Then don't tell her. We can say we're going for a drive and just happen to stop there and check it out."

"Sneaky. But you know, it just might work. Why don't you phone her and tell her we're coming over? We'll see what happens."

An hour later, we pulled up in front of Mom's house. Draya waited in the van while I went to the door. Mom was ready, jacket done up, purse on the chair.

"Why doesn't Draya come in to see me?" Mom complained, looking past me to the van. "She never comes here. Doesn't she like my house?"

"Draya can't get into your house, Mom. All those steps make it impossible with her wheelchair."

Mom stared at me, then at the van outside. Her eyes rested on the eight steps leading to her front door. "That's why she never comes to visit," she said with surprise. "I wondered. But of course. She can't get in."

Draya had been in a wheelchair over ten years now. *How long has Mom actually suffered from dementia, Lord? How long did she manage to hide it?*

Mom handed me her keys to lock the door and hurried to the van to see her granddaughter. I helped Mom navigate her way up the side ramp where she paused to give Draya a hug before taking her seat in the back. I helped buckle her in, and then broached our plan.

"Mom, Draya's wondering if we could drive by Klassen Manor, that place you were reading about in the *Edmonton Seniors* paper."

Mom hesitated, but I could see her looking at Draya with love. I had never known her to say no to her granddaughter.

I wonder if we're being manipulative? But does it matter if this is a chance to help Mom move forward?

As expected, Mom agreed. "I don't know where you're taking me," she said with a laugh. "You kids!"

Draya and Mom chatted while I prayed. *Your will be done, Lord. And I sure hope this place is your will!*

Klassen Manor had been built in a new suburb of the city. We pulled into the parking lot and surveyed the seniors home. The residence was shaped in a wide U with each apartment boasting a balcony.

"It's so high," Mom said in a shaky voice. "Do they make you live up there? There's four on top of each other. I couldn't be way up. There are fires."

Draya quickly countered. "Most of the apartments are lower, Grandma. But we're just looking, so not to worry. The grounds sure are nice. Look at the raised flowerbeds."

Several elderly, well-dressed women were puttering with the plants, pulling a few weeds, and chatting. The picture they made certainly matched the photo in the ad.

"Why don't we get out and stroll around the building," Draya suggested. "Just to see what the back looks like."

The day was warm and sunny, and the walk was pleasant. We sauntered past residents who were also enjoying the day, some with walkers, some with canes. "I'm glad I don't need something to help me walk. That would be horrible," Mom confided to Draya, her hand on the arm of the wheelchair. I chuckled. *Draya is so comfortable in her chair that people hardly even notice it.*

We completed our circuit and arrived at the entrance. Draya was casual. "Shall we go in? It's wheelchair accessible. Just push that big button, Grandma."

"What button? Oh, this?"

The double doors swung wide, welcoming us into an elegant foyer with a vaulted ceiling. Before us was a wide common area set with traditional furnishings, and to the right a dining room decorated in the style of a posh restaurant.

Midafternoon was a quiet time here. We tiptoed in, feeling a need to preserve the silence. A manager came out of a side office.

"Welcome," she said. "I'm Terry. Are you here to see the facility?" Mom was silent, her eyes large.

"Can we take a look?" Draya asked. "My grandma was wondering what your place is like."

"Why don't I show you around, then?" Terry positively glowed with enthusiasm.

I nodded vigorously. Draya fell in behind Terry, and Mom retreated two full steps. Grasping her arm gently but firmly, I brought her back into the group and the tour began.

An apartment on the top floor was empty, so our little party assembled in the elevator.

"If you lived here, Grandma, I could come and visit you. I can get around the whole place." Draya kept up a running monologue, pointing out the positives.

Mom hesitated as we stepped out of the elevator, but with my arm snug in hers, we followed our guide to the vacant apartment.

"This is a one-bedroom, facing east. You'd have morning sun here. The carpet's a bit stained. The last tenant left on short notice. We'll be cleaning the carpet before it's rented again."

Short notice? That's probably significant in a residence for seniors.

"Where do you put your things?" Mom asked, standing just inside the empty, open-concept space that echoed as we spoke. She turned in a slow circle and stopped, facing the kitchenette.

I opened the cupboards, six in all, and indicated the entry closet. "There'll be a closet in the bedroom, too," I said a little too brightly.

"What about the basement? I have things in the basement."

"We'd help you sort through what you want to bring, Grandma. The rest of it we can store somewhere."

"You go look in there," Mom waved Draya towards the bedroom. "I don't know if I can get in."

Mom's language is getting a little confused. This must be stressing her out. Still, we need to move forward.

We grouped around Mom and shuffled her into the bedroom, noted four walls, a closet and a window, then returned to the main space. I brought Mom to the patio door, which the manager opened. "You go," Mom indicated to Draya. "You see." "I can't get over the ledge, Grandma. You should look, though. I bet it's a good view." The manager and I stepped onto the balcony, but Mom showed no interest. After a moment of coaxing, we gave up and returned to the living room.

"When would she move in?" Mom asked the manager.

"When…who?"

"You move around so easily," Mom turned to Draya. "Would your friend live here too?"

"You mean my husband? No, Grandma. We're not moving here. Matt and I will stay in our house. But if you moved here, we could come and visit."

Perhaps Mom felt safer thinking Draya would move here. From that point on, the conversation deteriorated quickly. We continued to attempt to engage Mom, but it appeared her only goal was to escape the place. An hour later we left with a stack of brochures, menus, activity planners and an application. "If you decide to join us, Nancy, be sure to call," the manager's voice lilted.

Safe in the van, Mom suddenly began talking with unexpected enthusiasm. "Did you see those ladies at the tables? There were big windows. They talked. I think they were happy. And the library. So many books. Do you have to buy them? Is it a store?"

"The residents can borrow books whenever they want. Remember she said they're all large print? That would be useful."

"That restaurant is so big."

"It's more like a dining room," I explained. "Do you remember you said once that it would be nice to go someplace close to have a meal? Well, that's exactly what this would be. They provide three meals a day, and it's all included in the cost."

"Well, what if you don't eat? Do they pay you back?"

"No, I don't think it works that way."

"Well, that's not right. That's taking money without service. They cheat."

"There was that nice beauty salon right there in the building," Draya quickly changed the subject. "That would be really handy."

"I can never get to my hairdresser's when she's open," Mom ruminated. "This one would be open."

Back at home, I opened the van door to help Mom out.

"Don't forget the information package," I said, indicating the folder on the seat. Mom picked it up and placed it on Draya's lap.

"No, Grandma. You keep this. I'm not planning to move, but you might want to consider it. This information is for you to look at. See if it's a place you'd like to live."

Mom laughed and tucked the package under her arm. Smiling as though she'd had a grand time, she gave both of us hugs and said goodbye.

I wonder, Lord. Is this the place for Mom? She's the one who picked it out. She seemed pleased with what she saw, well, sort of. I guess time will tell.

A month later, Mom was still perusing the Klassen Manor information package.

"Would you like to go and visit again?" I asked one day. "Take another tour?"

"It's before, you know. People have to sometimes. You can't always not. You just have to."

I decided to interpret her comments in the affirmative.

"We could go next week," I suggested. "Shall I phone and book a time?" I didn't say it, but my hope was to strike while the proverbial iron was hot.

"The airport won't close down yet. That money has to go somewhere."

Ignoring this, I broached a new idea. "You know, you could afford to try the place if you wanted to. You've managed your money really well. There's enough in your savings along with your pension income to easily cover the cost if you wanted to check it out. Like a trial period. You could move into Klassen Manor and see if you like it, but keep the house for the time being. Rick and I would take care of it for you. If you don't like apartment living, you could move back here."

"Would you do that?" she asked, looking both surprised and grateful. "I don't have to sell the house?"

"If you liked living there, then you could sell the house later. But you don't have to sell it first. You have enough money in the bank to keep the house and pay rent at Klassen Manor at the same time."

"What about here? Are you going to move in then?"

"No. Rick and I will stay in our house. But we'll take care of yours—the lawn, the weeds, stuff like that. Then if a few months go by and you'd don't like it at Klassen, you could move back."

"Where would we all sleep? Will you and Rick sleep downstairs?"

"No. Rick and I are staying in our house."

"I think we should talk about living together. That would be a good idea. But we have to all sit down and talk about it. We'd have to know that we might fight sometimes. People fight but it doesn't mean anything. You could go downstairs and get away."

The conversation had veered sideways, irretrievable now. Reluctantly I dropped the discussion.

That evening, though, I called Lawrence to discuss the matter. "I think we need to make a strong effort to nudge Mom forward on this plan of hers," I recommended.

"I agree. She's showing interest, so we should help her achieve her goal. Why don't you see if you can get her to visit again, and fill out the application. I'll be coming up in a few weeks. We can follow up then."

Yes, Lord, we can follow up then. Please prepare Mom's heart and mind for this move. Help her be open to the necessary changes. Guide me in taking her through the rental steps as slowly or as quickly as is right for her.

As I prayed, a verse from scripture filled my mind: "There is a time for everything, and a season for every activity under the heavens"(Ecclesiastes 3:1). I smiled. This was definitely confirmation. *This feels right, Lord. Help us move forward, I pray.*

Time is a great revealer of truth, however. It would be several weeks before I understood the degree to which I was deluding myself.

Klassen Manor Flip Flop

"You look very smart," I remarked to Mom when I picked her up for her second tour of Klassen Manor. She was dressed in a crisp pink shirt, tucked neatly into navy slacks that I knew were at least fifteen years old. A soft pink chiffon scarf was tied at her neck and tucked into the shirt, giving her a professional look.

"Are you sure? I don't want to look poor."

"You don't look poor at all," I assured her.

As we drove, Mom kept up a fretful commentary which I countered at every turn. "It's a very long way, isn't it?" she said.

"It's easy to get to, though. The freeway makes it very direct."

"What if I have to go to the bank?"

"They have a bus that takes the residents to their banks once a week. You can go to the TD branch near Klassen Manor."

"I don't know why you think this is a good idea," she said.

"You're the one who chose this place, Mom. Remember the ad in the *Edmonton Seniors*? You've been looking at it for months. I think it's only right that we explore it fully."

I didn't add that I had my chequebook with me, in case we got to the point where Mom might choose to place a deposit on an apartment.

Pulling into the parking lot, we were granted a panoramic view of the majestic, sprawling building, only a few years old. The landscaping was pristine, trees and flowerbeds perfectly placed, with additional colour spilling from flowerboxes on many of the balconies. It looked luxurious.

I turned to Mom, ready to remark on the grandeur, and was startled to see that, tiny as she was, she seemed to shrivel before my eyes. "Do you think I could really live in a place like that?" she asked, her voice quavering.

"I think it would be a great place to live." Even to my ears, my words sounded like a radio ad. "They have the beauty salon right on site. And there's a bus that will take you to the store every week. They have all those activities, and the lovely dining room."

"But I don't have anything nice enough to wear."

With a flash of understanding, I realized Mom was looking at the Manor through the eyes of her childhood. As a little girl, her family had suffered greatly during the Depression, forced to live on government handouts for several years. As a wife and mother, there were periods during which our family had struggled financially. Mom had felt it her responsibility to hide our shameful state and pinched every penny until we were solvent again. As a divorced career woman, she had managed her money with great care to ensure she would never be financially vulnerable again. Now she had more than enough to live comfortably, but it seemed that in her mind she had never moved from poverty to security.

As quickly as this revelation revealed itself, I rejected it, along with any looming implications. If this door to Klassen Manor was open a crack, I was prepared to shove it open as wide as possible.

"We'll just go and buy you some nicer clothes," I assured Mom. "And what you're wearing today is lovely. You look very nice."

"Do you think so?"

"Yes, I do. Come on. Let's go see what we can learn."

I helped Mom across the parking lot and we entered the massive foyer, with its vaulted ceiling, marble tile, and burgundy and gold colour scheme. The manager glided from her office, hand outreached to greet us. Once again we toured the facility, viewing the amenities and the apartment a second time. The unit on the fourth floor was still available. This time, Mom braved an excursion out onto the balcony. As we gazed across the garden to the freeway in the distance, I heard a loud humming. Directly below us were over a dozen air conditioning units, whirring against the heat.

No wonder this apartment is still vacant. Mom's hearing is so poor, though, I don't think this would bother her. It's bright and open. The paint's in good condition, and they say the carpet will be cleaned before possession. If she decides to take it, I added as an afterthought as we stepped back into the living room.

"I'll leave you here to look around," the manager said and discreetly made her exit.

Left to my own devices, I took over the job of salesperson, proclaiming the obvious benefits of apartment living.

Mom shuffled about, trying to get on board. "Where will I put my things? My papers?" she worried. I pointed to a wide shelf at the top of the closet.

"Will there be enough light? There's no light in the living room."

"You don't have a light in your living room now, Mom. We'll bring your lamps, and we could get another lamp, if you need it."

"It's up so high," Mom fretted. "What if there's a fire?"

"Remember we looked at the fire escape plan beside the elevator? They're all set up to deal with that if it happens."

Nervously, Mom raised barriers. Steadfastly, I dismantled them. Tiring of the effort, we took the elevator back to the lobby. The manager was ready and waiting. Her solicitous attitude brought to mind an attentive funeral director. I quickly shook off the image.

"If you'd like to look at an application, you could sit over here in the residents' snack area and have some privacy. Help yourself to refreshments." She indicated the counter with beverage carafes, bowls of fruit and packaged cookies. "Take all the time you need. I'll be in the office." She smiled, almost bowing, and slipped away unobtrusively, leaving us to our task.

"Coffee?" I asked.

"Oh, yes. Please."

I filled a cup for each of us, chose some chocolate chip cookies, and joined Mom in a booth.

Did I actually ask Mom for her decision? I'm sure I must have. Soon I was filling in the information as Mom watched and sipped her coffee.

The manager returned. I wrote a cheque for five hundred dollars as a down payment, and Mom signed the rental agreement.

The afternoon was waning as we returned to the car. During the drive I reminded Mom several times that we were not getting rid of her house. I told her she could give Klassen Manor a three-month trial. I reminded her that it was a month-to-month lease and she could give notice any time. We'd help her move back if she didn't like it.

When we arrived at her house I handed her the paperwork to review. "Once you've read it a few times, I'm sure you'll start to feel more comfortable with your decision," I told her, giving her a hug goodbye.

Heaving a sigh, I returned to the car, and made my own way home. *Was I pushing, Lord? Okay, yes. I know I was, a bit. Well, maybe more than a bit. Lawrence and I talked about this, though. We're afraid that if we leave it until Mom's completely ready, she'll never make the move. She just can't seem to get over that hump and take the leap. This is the place she's picked out, so I pray we're doing the right thing in nudging her enough to make it happen. And yes, if she's miserable, she can always go back to her house. I place the plans in your hands, Lord. May your will be done.*

"I'm arriving Thursday," Lawrence told me on the phone that evening. "If you make an appointment at Klassen, I can take Mom again and let her show me around. Another visit would probably be worthwhile."

"Good idea. I'm at my conference in Red Deer from Wednesday to Sunday, so we can connect when I get back to town."

I called Klassen Manor and arranged for Lawrence and Mom to have one more visit before preparing to take possession on the first. I was glad to be getting away for a few days. I'm a glutton for information, so a conference, even if it was work-related, would be pleasant.

My time away was uneventful, and I looked forward to hearing how Lawrence and Mom had made out. Sunday afternoon I joined the weekend travellers and made my way from Red Deer back to

Edmonton. During the drive I planned out the timeline for moving Mom to her new place.

We can leave most of Mom's stuff at the house. Not having to empty it takes much of the pressure off. We'll only need enough furniture to fill the bedroom and living room. Her kitchen table and chairs will fit in. A few dishes, her clothes, some of her papers, but not all. The rest can stay where it is. I'll call Monday and reserve a truck. What was the phone installation process? I'd better call about that as well.

After putting my suitcase away, I filled Rick in on the conference details, and he politely feigned interest. After hearing about his week at work, I asked my burning question.

"Did you hear from Lawrence?"

"Yes. He left a message Friday afternoon, saying he was going to Calgary to visit his kids."

"Friday? But that was when he was to take Mom for another visit at Klassen. And help her figure out what she would be taking with her to the apartment. You're sure it was Friday?"

"Very sure."

"Oh no. I hope things didn't go sideways…" *Lord, should I call Mom and see what happened? Should I call Lawrence? Should I sit here and do nothing? I don't think I can face a confusing conversation with Mom, and Lawrence knows I'm getting home today.*

Taking the path of least resistance, I chose option three—nothing.

"Rick, do you want some soup and toast?"

"Sounds good. I'll make the toast."

The doorbell rang as we finished our lunch. Rick cleared the dishes and I opened the front door.

"Lawrence! Are you okay?" My brother stood on the front step, shoulders slumped like a man defeated. Maggie flew by me, pawing at his shins. He bent and stroked her little body that wagged in excitement.

"I'm just on my way through from Calgary. I wanted to stop for a quick visit with you and Rick. Then I'm going home."

"Not seeing Mom?"

"I wish I could." He came in and I closed the door.

"Go on out to the deck," Rick offered. "I'll bring some drinks."

Lawrence and I sat in the shade of the awning. Maggie leaped to his lap and his hands took up the soothing action once again. Soon Rick joined us and we settled back to hear this latest tale.

"I haven't told Mom I'm back in town. I didn't say I was going to Calgary either. I just left."

"It didn't go well?"

"It didn't go well," he echoed. Maggie rolled over on his lap and Lawrence focused on her pink belly and vibrating paws.

"So," he tried to begin. After a few moments he made a second attempt. "So. The appointment was all set up. I thought everything was a go, that this was just one more reconnaissance trip. We went into the place. Very nice, by the way. The manager was ready. Took us up to the apartment and left us there. And bang. It was like she'd been preparing. She dug her heels in and said *absolutely not*. She could never live in a place like that. She was adamant. I didn't even try to argue. We went back down in the elevator. I cancelled the application and arranged for them to mail the deposit back to you."

"But she seemed on board. Did she give any reason?"

"Not really. Said we were forcing her, bullying her to live in this castle, and who did we think we were, telling her how to live her life. Stuff like that. Fine. I took her home."

"So when did you go to Calgary?" I still wasn't sure how all this had played out. Lawrence had arrived Thursday evening and the visit to Klassen had been booked for three o'clock Friday afternoon. What had transpired next?

"Calgary? I escaped that same evening. About two hours later, in fact."

"Escaped? Oh no." *Oh no* seemed to be my mantra these days. "Okay. Carry on."

"After we got back from Klassen Manor, she wanted groceries. I zipped out to Safeway and got what she'd asked for. When I got back she'd locked both the front and back doors. I knocked and knocked, but she wouldn't answer. My key to her place was in my bag in the house."

I remembered Mom saying she would never answer the door unless she was expecting someone, that you never knew who it might be. "Do you think she forgot you were coming back?" I asked.

"I have no idea," Lawrence sighed. "Finally I phoned her on my cell, long distance roaming charges of course, and she answered the phone. I told her I was outside and could she please let me in. She did, but she was huffy about it. Remember the time she locked me in the basement? I wasn't going through that again, so I left the groceries, grabbed my bag from the suite, said goodbye and headed off to Calgary."

"You're not going to check in with her then?"

"No," he sighed. "I know it's a cop-out, but I'd rather drive eight hours today than go and face her again. What I wish I could do is stop in and have an hour's visit and a cup of coffee. But she won't allow that. She lays on so much guilt," he said sadly. "She tells me I should be there more. I should come and put a new roof on her house. She needs new carpet and I should do that, too."

"But if she's planning to move at some point, doing all those repairs…"

"Oh, no. She's not going anywhere now. She's sure of that."

"But she had that realtor, Flanagan, come last spring. I thought she was intent on selling. She keeps saying she can't manage the upkeep on her own, that it's too much. And she's right."

"I know." Lawrence closed his eyes and leaned back in the patio chair. "All that's gone by the wayside. Here's her plan, as of Friday. Well, actually, I think she's been planning it since you last took her to see the apartment. Anyway, she has it all figured out.

"I'm to come and stay with her. Hire a contractor to put a new roof on the house and garage, and then get a new carpet installed. The old one is forty years old, and it's wrinkled and bumpy from that flood last winter. She tried to make me walk around on it to prove her point, like I wasn't believing her. I said I believed her, just that it wasn't practical and I wasn't going to do it.

"As for moving in with her for a few weeks while the work gets done, forget it. I could never come and stay for more than a night anymore."

For the first time, Rick spoke up. "You're always welcome to stay here, you know."

Lawrence smiled gratefully. "I know, and I thank you for that. My plan was always to stay with Mom and get as much visiting time as possible. Now, I don't know where things stand."

"I'm glad you could go and visit Shaemus and Joanne and the little girls," I interjected. "Nothing like unconditional granddaughter-love to soothe the soul."

"No kidding. They were great. A short visit, but a good one."

"And now you've driven three hours from Calgary and you're planning to do the five hours home from here? Why don't you spend the night at least?"

"I feel too guilty being in town and not seeing Mom. Thanks, but no. I'll go home."

An hour later Lawrence had said his goodbyes and was on the road, his heart still heavy. Rick went to putter in the garage, and I sat quietly on the deck, not knowing what to do next.

⁂

Lord, we need your help. This is a woman who floods her house. She's unable to cook anymore. She lives on cheese, yogurt, bread, bananas and tea with canned milk. And chocolate. Is it right for us to try to support her to live independently when clearly she can't? How much are we able to do to keep her safe, to keep her neighbours safe? What if she used the stovetop and set the house on fire? Bad enough that she would be injured, but there are houses on either side.

Here I am trying to figure things out again. I carry this burden a lot, and I know I don't have to. I wonder if I'll ever figure out how to truly surrender and live in the moment, trusting you implicitly. Lord, forgive my tendency to try to arrange not only my life, but another's as well. Help me recognize when I'm taking control, and cast my cares on you. On my own, I'd be a quivering mess at this point, but I'm not on my own. You are with me. You know what's happened, what's happening, and what's to come. You are my resource. My rock. My fortress. In you, I trust.

Haircuts and Patience

$\mathcal{I}$ wasn't sure Mom would answer when I called the next day, but she picked up the phone on the second ring. "You're calling just in time. Can we go for groceries?"

Shopping was uneventful. Mom's small grocery list was purchased and the items put away. As usual, we indulged in a cinnamon bun and ice cream at her kitchen table. I wondered if Mom would bring up the Klassen Manor fiasco. I wondered if I would bring it up.

Neither of us did.

A haircut was the topic of concern, however.

"Every time I walk to April's shop it's closed. I walk all the way there. Eight blocks. I count. And it's always closed."

"Where's April's shop? Is that the name of the salon?"

"Salon? April is the hairdresser. On the corner on Whyte Avenue. I walk there. It's always closed."

Mom's wavy, steel grey hair was indeed long and unkempt. I hesitated, feeling a little miffed that it seemed I was expected to deal with this mundane task as well.

Lord, why do I have to offer? Can't Mom call me if she wants me to book an appointment for her?

I was startled by a realization. It had been weeks since Mom had initiated a call, either to me or to Lawrence. Could she even manage the phone anymore?

"Where do you get your hair cut?" she asked as I continued to hesitate.

"There's a hairdresser near my house. Would you like me to book you in for an appointment?"

"When?"

"I'll call when I get home. I'll let you know when she has an opening."

"How do I get there?"

"I'll take you."

"Will you? Oh, you're so good to me. What would I do without you?"

My mouth formed an insincere smile. Mom got up and gave me a hug. I left her standing on the front step, waving me goodbye.

As promised, I booked an appointment for Mom's haircut and called her the next morning to let her know the time.

"How are you doing today?" I asked when she picked up the phone.

"Oh, well. You know. You can't be sure," she muttered.

"I called the hairdresser," I told her. "Are you up for getting a haircut tomorrow?"

"A haircut? What are you talking about, a haircut. As if you cared about anyone's hair."

Whoops! What just happened? Did I miss something?

"Are you still wanting a haircut, Mom?"

"You, pretending a haircut matters. You and your brother. You're both just after this house. How much am I worth, your brother says. He thinks this is all his. And you two talking behind my back, planning all this…"

I half-listened to her tirade as I considered what I was hearing.

There it is again, Lord. She's remarkably articulate when her words are fuelled by anger. This puts me in mind of last spring when she tore a strip off me, thinking I'd tricked her into getting keys cut for her house. Somehow I don't feel drawn into her paranoia this time. That's good, isn't it?

Mom carried on. "When you get all that money, what are you going to do with it? You and your brother. Are you going to have parties? With my money? Just have a grand old time?"

On the phone, she seems to forget she's talking to a real person. It's as though the thoughts that fill her mind when she's alone come roaring out. Rarely does she speak to me this way when we're face to face. In person, she sees me as a helper, someone who's earned her trust. When we're apart, she doesn't seem to remember that.

I wonder if she talks out loud to herself about these accusations she's making? I wonder if she rehearses them, and that's why she's so articulate?

My thoughts wandered, exploring possibilities as I let Mom's rant dissipate. After a time I broke in as she was taking a breath.

"So, do you want to get your hair cut tomorrow?"

There was silence for a moment, and then calmly she asked, "What time is the appointment?" Very proper and sensible again, just like that.

"Three o'clock. I'll pick you up about two-thirty if that works for you."

"Two-thirty is fine," she said. "I'd better write it down. Just a minute," she paused. "Two-thirty. Today?"

"Tomorrow."

"Tomorrow," she confirmed.

Another pause.

"Mom, I love you."

"Well, I'll try to be more lovable tomorrow."

"Okay," I smiled. "'Bye."

⌒⧞⌒

Mom was almost ready when I arrived the next day. I slipped into a chair and sat quietly, observing her actions.

My inclination is to chat as Mom finishes gathering her stuff, but I know I can't engage her when she's getting ready. If I stay quiet, she can follow her train of thought, even if it goes off track a bit. It's not easy, though. In fact, it feels rude. Small talk may be our societal norm, but it doesn't fit in Mom's world anymore, not unless she's sitting still.

I waited in the kitchen, consciously maintaining my silence. Mom wandered to the table. "My purse. I think I left it here." She sat down and looked at the empty chair across from me. Her eyes moved to the table and locked on the list she'd reviewed in great detail with Rick several weeks before.

"That's my checklist," she offered. "I do that every night. I go around the whole house."

Suddenly she rose, beckoning me to follow. We circled the main floor and noted each lamp cord that was unplugged, each tap that needed to be turned off. She pointed to the stove dials. "These, too. I know they don't work, but I check them anyway."

Then we were off to the porch where she demonstrated locking the back door, turning the key several times. Next we made our way down the steps.

Lord, the clock is in your hands. Let Mom get this out of her system, and help us get to the hairdresser's on time.

After a tour of the basement taps, cords, and furnace pilot light I followed her back upstairs.

I really need to bite my tongue, Lord. Every fibre of my being wants to remind Mom that we have an appointment. The clock is ticking. Trying to hurry her up, though, is counterproductive. Nope, Lord, keep my mouth quiet, and my attitude patient.

It was 2:45 when, just as suddenly as the tour began, it ended, and she was back on track.

"Why are we standing around? Don't we have to be somewhere?"

"We do, and we have just enough time to get to the hairdresser's without rushing," I said, relaxing.

The rest of the afternoon was pleasant in its normalcy. The beauty salon was quiet, so arriving at 3:05 wasn't a concern. I'd been coming to Avonmore Beauty Salon for several years. Mom and the hairdresser, Chano, chatted amiably as I flipped through old magazines. I was thankful for the beautician's gentle manner as she showed great interest in everything Mom had to say. As I half-listened, I realized Mom's comments were nothing more than a string

of polite conversational clichés. Still, they gave the illusion of awareness and engagement.

"The weather's been quite something," she noted. *Not nice. Not
bad. Generic.*

"Is this a good place to work?"

"Everything's so clean."

"My hair keeps growing."

I recalled reading on the Internet that professional people are
often able to mask their level of dementia by accessing phrases that
make them appear more aware than they are. I realized this was the
case with Mom. Having been a teacher, she was able to give the semblance of conversation using generic phrases.

Mom was beaming as she put on her coat and made her way to
the door. I quietly handed Chano some cash as it was clear that that
piece of the transaction had slipped from Mom's awareness.

"Shall we go to Albert's at Bonnie Doon Mall for a snack?" I
asked.

"I can show off my new haircut," Mom proclaimed. "I'll buy you
a piece of lemon meringue pie as a treat."

Bobbi and Nancy enjoying a treat

Later, as we drove back to Mom's house, she reached out and put her hand on my arm. "You are a very nice person."

I was touched. "Thanks, Mom. I think you're a very nice person too. I know you have a lot of struggles these days, but you never give up. That's impressive."

"I don't know about that. I get pretty bad. And I can't think. And I can't remember. I am so stupid…"

"No, not stupid, Mom. Your brain just doesn't work as well as it used to. But you're finding lots of ways to get around that. That's smart."

We drove the rest of the way in silence, and I dropped her at the curb in front of her house. I wanted to watch to be sure she made her way up the steps. Doggedly, Mom stood on the sidewalk, waiting for my car to leave.

Mom won and raised her hand in salute as I drove away.

⸎

Lord, on days like today, when the sun is shining, when I've managed to be patient, and Mom has accomplished something she feels good about, it seems to both of us that we're succeeding in stemming the progress of dementia, that she can remain in her home.

Then I look back just two days ago and remember her fury when I called to tell her about the hair appointment.

Something has to break, Lord. It's September. Snow could be here by October. I think another winter trapped in her house will destroy Mom's sanity. Maybe mine, as well.

Jesus, help us, I pray. Show me, show Mom, show someone what we should do before something drastic happens. Until then, I will wait.

hree weeks and no contact, Lord. I'm struggling with the same inner battle. On one side, I'm relieved that every time I pray and ask if I should call Mom, you make it clear I'm to wait a little longer. On the other side, I feel guilty because I know I'm relieved that I don't have to face her. That seems selfish and unkind.

Why is it so hard to interact with Mom?

I guess it's reasonable that I don't want to call and get yelled at. That doesn't always happen, though. Usually she works hard to be pleasant and get along. It is a stretch to take her out. Pretending normalcy is exhausting. I have to be conscious of where to position myself, what tone to use, what might confuse her. I'm constantly trying to set things up so she can feel successful and not "stupid," as she's quick to say when she does something wrong. Conversation is a chore when I have to decode her sometimes garbled communication. I've never been good at small talk and neither has Mom. These days, it leaves both of us drained.

I guess you're right, Lord. There really is nothing simple about interacting with Mom. Every moment with her is work.

But no contact for three weeks? Okay. I'm trusting her in your hands. Please knock me over the head when you want me to call. Until then, I'll "Keep Calm and Carry On." I hear that's what Winston Churchill planned to tell the Brits if the UK was invaded by Germany. This isn't quite the same level of concern, but it feels like a battle nonetheless.

⌐∞ჼ

I took another sip of steaming coffee and opened a document on my computer. I was enjoying the Saturday morning I had set aside to read through the submissions our writing group would be reviewing that afternoon. *Lord, thank you for this peaceful day. A quiet morning of reading what my fellow writers have created, a stimulating afternoon of discussion with them, and a relaxing evening with Rick...*

The phone rang. I glanced at the clock. 10:00 a.m. Did Draya need something? I looked at the call display. *Whyte Hall.* The name was familiar. Wasn't that the Assisted Living residence beside Mom's hairdresser, the salon she said was always closed?

"Hello?"

"Hello. My name is Luba. You are related to Nancy Bastion?" a heavily accented voice asked.

What is this? A marketing call?

"Yes," I replied cautiously, "I'm her daughter."

"I work at Whyte Hall. Your mother arrive here fifteen minutes. She is very pleasant, but I not sure what she want. I look in her purse and find your number. There is money in there too. I push that aside. I don't touch it. And she have a bag of mail."

"I'll be right there," I told her. "Ten minutes."

"Thank you."

I fired off a quick email to our writing group, explaining I might be late. Or might not arrive at all. I had no idea what to expect.

Whyte Hall Seniors' Residence is in Mom's neighbourhood but I couldn't imagine her going there on purpose. Her friend Winnie had lived there for several years. Mom had told me horror stories of visits to her friend who had suffered from Parkinson's. She described how a nurse would force pills between Winnie's lips and hold her hand over Winnie's mouth until she swallowed, how they treated her rudely and drugged her, in Mom's words "like an animal." Winnie had passed away ten years ago. Why Mom would show up there I couldn't begin to imagine.

Thinking wouldn't answer my questions, and it occurred to me that Mom might not be able to answer them either. Praying for discernment, I zipped through the Saturday morning traffic and found a parking space in front of Whyte Hall. A large sign announced *Assisted Living for Seniors. Newly Renovated. Under New Management.* That, at least, was hopeful.

I stood in the entryway, stymied. You needed a security code to be admitted. I could see the office, but it was Saturday and no staff were present. A sign taped by the inside door warned, "Do not let anyone you do not know into the building."

Just then an elderly lady with a walker noticed me. I smiled encouragingly and she pushed the button from her side, opening the door. Stepping into the lobby, I tried to get my bearings. To the right was a large, empty dining room. Before me were two elevators. On the left, a wide hallway led to a busy common area.

And there was my mother, sitting poised and proper, in a straight-back chair. Two little boys of two or three years of age were playing with trucks as their parents visited with, I presumed, their grandfather. A happy, homey atmosphere filled the room as other residents made their way back and forth, some watching a large screen TV, others working on a puzzle.

My eyes rested on Mom.

She was dressed in her best plaid blazer, purchased more than two decades before during her teaching career. Now it hung loosely, a little off-centre on her shrunken frame. Her pink chiffon scarf was tied neatly around her neck, giving that professional touch. Her grey hair was askew. On her lap she clutched her ever-present purse and a small brown Starbucks bag stuffed with papers. She watched the activities with interest, a pleasant smile on her face.

I took a seat next to her chair. "Hi Mom."

"Well, you know," she said, as though I'd stepped into a conversation already in process. "Sometimes you have to do something. You can't leave it and leave it."

"Did you walk over here, Mom?" I asked. The weather was nice, but an eight-block walk is quite a distance for a ninety-one-year-old. "I have my mail." She showed me the Starbucks bag. I did a quick inventory. Inside were some bills, a few unopened envelopes of junk mail, several blank pieces of old graph paper and some carefully cut pieces of cardboard. "I have enough money, I think, but if I don't, can you take care of it?"

A caregiver in a light blue uniform spotted me and came to join us. "You are daughter?" she said, relief evident in her voice. I smiled and nodded. "I am Luba. Your mother she come to the door. Someone we let her in. I ask her if she is visiting but she does not say who. I look in her purse for a name and number. There is list there that say your name and phone, so I phone it. I do not touch the money. There is a lot of money."

At the mention of money, Mom considerately opened her purse, holding it wide for me to see. It appeared there might be upwards of a thousand dollars loosely stuffed in the gaping cavity. I understood the compromising position Luba had found herself in.

Suddenly things began to fall in place. "Mom," I asked. "I just want to clarify. Are you saying you came here this morning because you'd like to move in here? Move away from your house and come to live here at Whyte Hall? Is that right?"

Ignoring me, Mom turned to Luba. "There's just a time, you know. Things can't last forever. You don't always know, now, do you? That child seems happy." Mom smiled again at the toddler, playing with his grandparent. "It's nice here."

I listened closely as Mom exchanged a disjointed conversation with Luba. It seemed that my estimation was correct. Mom had decided to move to a location of her choice, and one that was in her own neighbourhood. Across the street was her Safeway. Next door was her pharmacy, and her bank was situated just down the block. Most importantly, Mom had carried out the plan on her own.

I tuned back in to see if I could understand what she was telling Luba. The kind caregiver was struggling to decode Mom's sentences, but it became clear to me that Mom had been assessing her situation during the weeks the Lord had insisted I leave her alone.

"Trapped. It's ice and snow that traps old people," she explained to Luba. "All the days. All the nights. Anytime you want and you can't because you can't. Then crazy. Just crazy!" She indicated her temple, tapping hard, shaking her head is despair. "Then it was lost. The door. And the walls. They weren't here anymore." This time she tapped her forehead and I remembered her call last spring when she'd lost the image of her own house in her own mind.

Luba did a quick survey of her charges, making sure no one needed her attention. I was grateful for her patience with this stranger off the street.

Now Mom raised the brown Starbucks bag, pulling items out, waving them emphatically. "Always more and then before so much. To sort them. Who can? But the government will call. You never know when." It seemed she was saying there were many papers she felt she needed to manage. The fact that some were needed for tax purposes made them intimidating as well. "It's quiet here," she said as the toddlers squealed in delight, chasing a ball across the floor. "So many people in my basement. All night long they do. I can't go out of the bedroom now. Ever. Day and night. I get hungry." It seemed the voices on her radio were now keeping her in her room during the day as well. "I'm desperate now," she suddenly burst out, her voice trembling. "Do you have food?"

Luba looked at a loss. Was Mom asking for a meal? It seemed to be the right moment for me to step in.

"Mom." I paused, waiting for her attention. "Mom?" It took a moment, and then her eyes caught mine. "You've been saying that when the time is right, you'd like to move to a place where you can get meals, where you don't have to worry about the house. Is the right time now? Is this the place you'd like to move to?"

Luba took the opportunity and slipped out of her chair. "I be there if you need me," she said quickly and moved away.

Mom gazed at our surroundings, the pleasant smile returning to her face. My eyes followed hers.

Look at this homey, middle-class, family oriented atmosphere. This is definitely a place where Mom would feel comfortable. Not that other highfalutin place.

So this is why Jesus hasn't let me call or visit or even help out with grocery trips this past month. It's taken that length of time struggling on her own for Mom to decide she can't wait any longer. If I'd kept stepping in and helping, I would have prolonged the process. Lord, I am so glad I managed to listen.

My face echoed the smile on Mom's lips.

Just then Luba returned, carrying a thick information package. "There is for you and Nancy to read if you like."

"Thank you so much," I said. "You've been a wonderful help."

"Do we need to go now?" Mom asked, holding the package close.

"Yes, Mom. We have what you came for. How about I drive you home. We'll have tea and we can read all about Whyte Hall."

"Of course we will." Mom beamed, rising. She shook Luba's hand, and waved goodbye to the children. "Have a good day. I'll see you soon," she said to each person she encountered as we made our way to the door. I remembered how we had tiptoed into Klassen Manor, the Castle as Mom had labelled it. In contrast, the atmosphere here invited chitchat and greetings.

Back in Mom's kitchen, we devoured the information with excitement and talked about a plan.

"You need to take notes so you know what she talked about."

My brow furrowed for a moment, and then I realized Mom was flipping her pronouns again. "You'd like me to write down what we've talked about so you can review them later?"

A green notebook was open at the end of the table. I recognized my brother's handwriting. It seemed he'd been making notes for Mom as well. Turning to a clean page, I wrote out the plan in clear, plain language.

"I need to go to the bathroom. Will you wait?" Mom asked.

"Of course. Take your time." I'd given up watching the clock. If I missed my meeting, so be it. This was much more important.

I flipped back to Lawrence's list in the notebook. It was titled "What I'm Worth," followed by a list of Mom's assets: her house, her GIC's, her savings account balance.

What had Mom said when I'd called her about the hair appointment? Something about Lawrence and I wanting her house, and Lawrence believing this was all his.

The light dawned. Lawrence had written, "What I'm Worth."

Lawrence had tried to make the list personal, as though Mom were writing it. Given Mom's difficulty with pronouns, however, she believed he was stating what he expected his inheritance would be, and she was upset because the assets were still hers.

With this important information at hand, I carefully worded the new information, trying to ensure Mom knew she would be in control every step of the way.

Together we worked through Whyte Hall's package.

The Plan, if Nancy Moves

Nancy has decided she wants to look into moving to Whyte Hall.

Bobbi will call Whyte Hall on Monday and make an appointment to have a tour.

Nancy will then decide if this is a place she wants to live.

If Nancy decides she wants to pursue living there, Bobbi will help her understand the details and go with her to any meetings Nancy wants her to attend.

Nancy will make the final decision as to whether she moves to Whyte Hall or not.

If Nancy decides to follow through with the application, she will need to visit a doctor to have the medical form filled out. Bobbi will arrange an appointment if Nancy so chooses.

If Nancy moves, her house can remain empty for up to a year. Nancy does not have to sell her house, even if she moves to Whyte Hall.

If Nancy moves, Lawrence will come and help Bobbi move the things she wants to take to her new apartment.

Nancy can make these decisions as quickly or as slowly as she wants. Nancy is in charge of all the decisions.

I finished The Plan and slid the notebook across the table. Mom looked it over and smiled. "You wrote that up so fast!" she exclaimed. I smiled back. "Okay, Mom. You study it, and if you have any questions, write them down. I'll call Whyte Hall on Monday and then call you about when we can go for a tour. Okay?"

"You're such a help," she said, hugging me. I picked up my purse and headed to my car. The clock on the dash said 11:45 a.m.

Could all of this have happened in less than two hours? Lord, how quickly the landscape can change when you're involved. To top it off, I have just enough time to get to my writing group. How perfect is that?

This feels so different from the Klassen Manor fiasco. Then, I was plotting and scheming, convincing Mom to move. This time, Mom has taken the lead. A miracle, in my books!

As I drove, however, practical concerns filtered in, and my conversation with Jesus became more intense.

If the move happens, how will Mom's brain be able to grasp the ins and outs of renting an apartment? Will she be able to understand the rules of a seniors' residence? She's lived in the same house for four decades. Will her brain be able to learn new routines, figure out how to navigate in a new space? How will she manage with a common laundry room?

Quickly, I checked my thoughts. *The future isn't my concern, is i,t Lord? I know Mom could back out again, so I'm not going to lock into this plan. If you keep things moving, I'm on board. Help me not to run ahead. May you and Mom take control.*

One thing, though. If Mom doesn't make this move now, I'm pretty sure another winter alone in her house will destroy her mentally. Just saying…

I trust her into your care.

Chapter Twenty-Nine

*L*awrence's cell rang several times before he finally picked up. I filled him in on Mom's excursion to Whyte Hall.

"I'm excited," I added when I'd given him all the details from the day before.

"We'll see," he said cautiously. "She's backed out of everything she's agreed to so far, including the things she put in motion herself. Remember home care? Remember the alert button? I guess we move forward, though. If we had Power of Attorney, it would be different, but as it is, she calls all the shots, no matter her mental state. She has all the power."

"I know. Like getting the medical. She seemed to understand about that. I've booked her an appointment with my doctor for Friday."

"It's been, what, twelve years now since the doctor refused to sign off on her driver's license unless she started taking blood pressure medicine?" he asked.

"At least that. And she hasn't seen a doctor since. She still says they're evil manipulators, out to get her money and fill her with drugs."

"I hope she can follow through on the appointment, then. It's a requirement before her application can be accepted, isn't it?"

"It is. I'll have to be careful not to get in the way of her making the right decisions," I said nervously. "Hopefully I won't blow it and upset her so she gets derailed."

"Don't worry about that, sister-of-mine. You're doing a fine job. I'm just sorry I'm so far away. I'm not of much assistance."

"The fact that you don't criticize what I'm doing is a big help," I said honestly. "I hear of other families who are constantly at odds with each other. Especially when there are siblings far away who think they know best how Mom or Dad should be managed. I'm glad we're in agreement with simply doing the best we can."

"Me too. Keep me posted. I hope it all goes well."

As I hung up the phone, I offered a quick prayer for the future.

Lord, may Rick and I not wait until "the time is right" to put our affairs in order. May we do it way in advance so our kids don't have to go through this emotional field of landmines someday.

⟡

So far so good. I called Whyte Hall, and they said we're welcome to come and tour the building any time during business hours. We'll get groceries at Safeway, then pop across the street for our visit.

We arrived as the dining room at Whyte Hall was beginning to fill for lunch.

"Look at all those wheel machines," Mom commented as yet another walker made its way past us. "Where do they put them all?"

Just then the manager, Lauren, arrived. Slender, with long brown stylish hair and red framed glasses, she looked too young to be in charge of a place this size. Her business-like manner belied her apparent youth, though.

"You must be Nancy." She shook Mom's hand. "Thank you for considering Whyte Hall. As we look around, if you have any questions, be sure to ask me."

Mom beamed. I knew she appreciated being treated professionally. It must have felt like the old days when her status as a teacher automatically brought respect. Together we followed Lauren to the fourth floor where two open units were available for viewing.

Mom didn't seem as anxious riding in the elevator this time. The apartments were much smaller than those at Klassen Manor. The fact that none had balconies seemed to be a plus. She enjoyed looking out the window onto the back alley, but didn't appear disturbed by the height.

We returned to the lobby where the manager invited us to take all the time we wanted to explore the main floor. Together we wandered around the common area and dining area. Lunch was still in progress, so we moved to sit next to the floor-to-ceiling windows near a cozy fireplace. From comfortable couches we watched passersby on the busy main street.

In the common area, we found a wall of large photographs depicting scenes from Edmonton's history—scenes that were part of Mom's youth. She took me through a story connected with each photo, telling me tales of her younger days in the city, speaking as though these were her pictures, and this was her home. I was very encouraged.

Back at her house, we talked more about all that moving would entail.

"Shall we make another list about what we'll have to do next?"

"You should know that by now," she said, sternly. "And don't make it silly like this one." She indicated my first list, *The Plan if Nancy Moves.* "Why would you write it like this, saying *Nancy* everywhere. I'm not a child. I know who this is about."

Don't let me comment, Lord. Keep my mouth shut.

"What shall I call this list?"

"Why do you have to call it anything? Just make a list."

"Just make a list. Good idea."

See the doctor on Friday.

"Who do I have to see?"

"It's a lady doctor that I've been to. She's young. Very nice."

"Oh, I'm glad it's a lady. That's much better."

2. Fill in and sign the application.

3. Decide what furniture to take.

"Who will move the furniture? You and Rick can't do all that."

"Should we book a moving truck?"

"Of course. I booked movers when I moved here. It's the only way to go."

"I agree," I said enthusiastically.

4. Book movers.

"When will you come back?" Mom asked after she'd read the list over.

"Friday. I'll be here at ten. We'll see the doctor, and then go for lunch. How does that sound?"

"Just perfect," she said with joy in her voice.

❧

The day was sunny, the sky blue. I bounced up Mom's steps, excited for the day's plan. Not so Mom. Her confusion was evident from the moment I walked in. "So when does this doctor arrive, or are you lying about that too?"

"The doctor is in Beaumont, Mom. We're going to drive there."

"What kind of plan is that? I thought you knew what you were talking about?"

My buoyant mood crashed like the proverbial lead balloon, and I gritted my teeth. "Let's just get going, okay? It's a half-hour drive."

Bitterly complaining, Mom donned a flowered jacket and picked up her purse. I did note that she had taken extra care to dress nicely and that her hair was combed.

Once in the car, she immediately went on the attack. "You said you're going on holidays tomorrow."

"Yes, Rick and I are going away for four days. Just a little break."

"And why are you doing that? Does Rick know?"

"Of course he knows. He's coming too." I navigated the busy roads until we turned onto the highway that would take us to the suburb where my doctor's office was located

Mom was like a dog with a bone.

"Of course Rick knows," she mimicked my words belligerently. "Of course he knows! Do the relatives know? If I called them would they not be surprised?"

"Which relatives?"

"Your brother's relatives. I can call them, you know."

"You mean Shaemus and Joanne? Yes, they know. We're staying with them when we go through Calgary. I told you that."

"Well, of course they're in on it. And your breath smells!"

Trapped together in the car, we drove for twenty-five excruciating minutes. Mom's rude comments and groundless accusations hurtled around the car's interior. I tried to pray, but to no avail. I tried to sing hymns in my head, again to no effect.

I will not get sucked into her vortex, Lord. I will not!

"Who knows why you think you want to see this doctor. What's he going to say about this?" she said.

"She. The doctor is a she."

"So you say. We should just turn around right now and go home. Why would you do this anyway?"

My brain disengaged. My emotions took charge, and I retaliated. "I took the day off work for this, Mom. All I'm trying to do is help you carry through with *your* plan to move to Whyte Hall. You are *not* going to back out of this."

As the words flew from my mouth, shame filled my heart. Had I really said that?

"I'm not discussing this any more," I announced. Mom continued to rant. To block the sound, I sang hymns out loud. Softly but out loud.

Once at the doctor's office, Mom sat quietly. Our wait was mercifully short. I had expected and dreaded that she would require a physical, but as it was a first appointment, the doctor let Mom sit in a comfy chair by her desk for a get-to-know-you chat.

Once again, Mom pulled out familiar phrases she could easily string together, giving a semblance of awareness.

"I see you're not on our system, Nancy. Has it been awhile since you've seen a doctor?"

"It's been so long, you know. I haven't been in ages."

"Can you tell me if you have pain anywhere, Nancy?"

"Oh goodness. Don't we all?"

I interjected and told the doctor that Mom used aspirin and milk of magnesia, but nothing else.

"Tell me, Nancy. What day is it today?"

"Today? Oh, well, we came to see you," Mom said with a nervous laugh.

"Do you know the year?" the doctor asked, pen poised.

"There are so many. I think I'm eighty-four now."

The doctor looked at Mom's date of birth on the form we'd given her to fill out. "Eighty-four? Or perhaps ninety-one?"

"Oh no, I'm sure it's not that big."

"Nancy, it seems to me you're in pretty good health for someone your age. I'm impressed. You've taken good care of yourself."

"I do. I take care. I walk."

"Walking is important." She made a notation on the form.

"I'm going to write down that you have mild diminished capacity. Do you understand?"

"I do get confused," Mom admitted. I was surprised that she understood what the doctor was saying.

"I'm going to sign off on this form for you, but I'd like you to book a full checkup. Will you do that?"

"Is that it?" Mom asked, surprised.

Is that it? I marvelled, just as surprised.

The doctor stood. "You have a good day, Nancy. You can book your next appointment at the desk."

I wonder if the doctor knows that we have no intention of coming back? She has to make the recommendation, but I think she understands that any further medical needs will be addressed through the doctors attached to Whyte Hall.

Thank you Lord for such an easy appointment. I'm so glad we didn't give up and turn around.

The drive back into the city was peaceful. Mom chatted and I relaxed. We stopped at Smitty's and shared a Denver sandwich. Mom excused herself to use the washroom, which was around the corner from our table. She got lost coming out, but a kind waitress helped her locate me. Distress quickly replaced the peace we'd achieved.

"I'm so stupid," Mom said repeatedly as we drove the rest of the way home.

I walked Mom into the house, to be sure she found her way safely. "I'm sorry I was so angry with you," she said, once her shoes and coat were off. "People have to be able to yell, though. Have to yell and get it out. We can't take it personally."

I didn't respond. I recalled when I was young how Mom would suddenly fly off the handle unexpectedly. Her lack of control during those times was frightening to me as a child. I realized it frightened me still.

Mom hung her coat in the closet.

"It's so cold now," she told me. "Come here. Look at this." She led me to the thermostat where I saw it was still turned all the way off. I recalled her mentioning the house was cold, but it hadn't occurred to me she might not have turned on the heat. It was the end of September and near freezing some nights.

"Well yes, it's cold. Your furnace isn't turned on." I reached out to adjust the thermostat. In a flash Mom slapped my hand away.

"Don't touch that!" In a tone she might have used with her elementary students, Mom lectured me. "The gas company has to come and do that. You can't just turn it on. This house is connected to every other house. They could all blow up."

I nodded in compliance. If I'd learned nothing else over the past year, I knew not to try to reason with dementia.

Calmer now, she went to the kitchen to put her purse away. Feeling just a smidgen of guilt, I turned up the thermostat and followed her.

Once again, Mom reviewed her safety checklist. "You go through both floors. You check the taps. You check the fire downstairs in the heater. You make sure the floor is level. And every plug has to be out. You don't worry about the dark, but you don't want to trip..."

Oh, Mom. Your caution is making your world smaller and smaller. I wish I could help you let go of some of the fear, but I don't know how.

I called later that evening, "Just checking to see if the house is still cold," I said.

"Well, I turned the thermostat down a bit. It is warmer now. Thank you."

So much for sneaking behind her back. I can't pull anything over on her.

"I didn't want you to freeze, Mom."

"And I didn't want to yell," she said contritely.

"We're good, Mom. I love you,"

"I love you too."

Lord, if you'd suggested ten years ago that Mom and I could be not only civil, but encouraging and loving towards each other, I'd have laughed in disbelief. Given our history together, I'd call this a miracle! Thank you for continuing to do a good work.

As promised, I called Lawrence and filled him in on the day's progress. "You should have heard how upset she was with Rick and me for going away this weekend. I couldn't believe it," I commented.

"You and Rick haven't gone away together and left her alone before," Lawrence pointed out astutely. "Last time you went on vacation, I came to spend the week. Maybe she's afraid she'll have no one to check up on her."

"I never thought of that! Poor Mom. I know. I'll get Draya to call her each day we're gone. Then she'll have contact if she needs anything."

"I'll call each day, as well. I think we can muddle through for four days. You deserve your break."

⁕

Lord Jesus, when I look back on the last two months, I see your hand at every turn. I tried to override all the signs that Klassen Manor wasn't right for Mom. I wanted so badly for her to move that I was willing to ignore both her and you. Thank you for stopping me from forcing a move that would have served to make only me more comfortable.

In contrast, each step of this Whyte Hall journey feels right, even though the road is definitely filled with potholes.

Please take good care of Mom while Rick and I are gone. And take good care of us, too.

Chapter Thirty

*R*ick and I drove through a grey drizzle on our way home from Canmore. I gazed out the window, marvelling at how four short days away from the chaotic pressures at home could be so rejuvenating. Autumn leaves had cushioned the trails as we strolled around Lake Louise and Banff. Summer tourists were gone and the ski crowds had yet to arrive so Rick and I had been able to explore the quaint shops and cafés in peace.

Lord, thank you for this period of rest. I think I'm ready for whatever is to come.

⌘

I re-read what I'd noted in my journal just a week earlier. "Ready for whatever is to come."

Ha! Famous last words. I'm already anxious about these next steps. Mom and I are to meet with the Whyte Hall manager today. Why is my heart so reluctant? Why can't I just take care of all these details without feeling like I'm dragging a dead weight behind me?

I paused in my morning devotions to let the dog out and to pour a second cup of coffee. Settling back in my rocker with my Bible on my lap, I hugged the hot blue mug and tried to be still.

Working out these arrangements on Mom's behalf, helping her figure out what's going on to make sure she's able to make sound decisions takes a lot of energy, mostly in not taking over and doing it myself. And there's always the added concern that she might back out at the last minute.

Okay. The dead weight is defined. What do I do with it?

Matthew 11:28 immediately came to mind. "Come to me, all you who are weary and burdened, and I will give you rest."

That's well and good, Lord, and I appreciate the sentiment. But how?

Just as quickly, another verse rose in my heart.

"Peace I leave with you; my peace I give you. I do not give to you as the world gives. Do not let your hearts be troubled and do not be afraid" (John 14:27).

Well, I'm not feeling your peace right now, so trying to figure things out isn't working. What can I do, then? I guess I could call Mom and tell her what time the meeting is.

I paused and took stock. Yes. That was a single, concrete step I could carry out.

Thank you, Lord. I'll do this one thing and leave the next piece to you.

c∞⁀

"Good morning, Mom. How are you doing today?"

"Well it's getting cold, you know. The house is. But no ice yet. I can still walk."

"I think it'll be a little while before the snow and ice come," I replied. "At least I hope so."

"So what's happening with this big thing of ours?"

Mom couldn't find the words to describe it, but I knew what she meant.

"I'm just calling to remind you that I've booked an appointment with the manager for this morning at ten. Does that still work for you?"

As usual, I asked Mom if the time was convenient. Even though she doesn't do anything more than sit in her house and wait for a distraction or obsess about worries, it seemed important to be as polite as I would with anyone else. If I ever let myself think of her as less than worthy of respectful treatment, I could become less than an appropriate

servant of Jesus in how I treat her. So I continued to behave as I would
have ten years ago.

"Today? Oh. Today. So it's ten o'clock I have to be there?"

I could hear trepidation in her voice. Was she worried she'd have
to go alone?

"Yes, ten o'clock. Can you be ready by nine-thirty? I'll pick you
up. We'll have lots of time to get there and find a parking space."

"Nine-thirty. Wonderful! Yes, let me write it down. Just a moment..." I heard fumbling before she came back on the line. "Will you
come in for tea afterwards?"

"That sounds lovely. I'll see you at nine-thirty."

"Nine-thirty today?"

"Yes. Today."

"Thank you," Mom said warmly. "Bye-bye."

I hung up the phone and sat back in the chair. My Bible sat closed
on my lap. One step completed, but I still felt something was dangling.

*Lord, show me what I need to understand from your word today,
what I need to understand before taking Mom to Whyte Hall.*

I opened to where I'd left off the day before, to the first chapter
in 2 John. Moments later I was reading verse six: "And this is love: that
we walk in obedience to his commands. As you have heard from the
beginning, his command is that you walk in love" (2 John 1:6).

I leaned my head back and closed my eyes.

Show me, Lord.

I remembered Mom's description of the people at the bank when
they ignored her, the customer, and talked to Lawrence instead. In
my heart I saw a picture of Mom stepping onto this path that would
result in leaving her home of forty years.

*Lord, this has to take such courage on Mom's part. She is old, un-
steady and unsure. She knows she can't trust her brain or her understanding of things. Yet she seems more determined at each step, even though
some, like the doctor's visit, are frightening. I don't know that Mom is a
believer, but it seems she's walking in obedience to your direction.*

What about me? My job is to walk alongside her in love, holding her gently by the elbow, providing a steadying hand, helping her move in the direction she chooses.

I breathed a deep, cleansing breath.

Thank you, Lord, for your peace. The outcome is in your hands. I don't have to worry, plan, push or decide. It's all up to you.

It's nine o'clock. Time to head out. Jesus, thank you for going before me. I know everything will occur according to your perfect plan. I'm just along for the ride.

☙

After the visit, I sent an email to Mom's grandkids:

"Grandma's adventure continues. We met with the manager at Whyte Hall. I asked lots of questions about cost, damage deposit, activities, etc. We established that it's a month-to-month rent, and she can give thirty days' notice at any time if she wants to leave. We looked at the fourth floor apartment again. It's still available, but someone else is considering it.

"When we left, we went back to her house and filled out the application. All the information, along with her bank statement and the doctor's report, are in a manila envelope. At any point now she can go there and say, 'I want to move in,' give them the papers and she's good to go.

"We talked about the moving process. I told her that Rick and I would help her carry it out if she decides to do this 'big thing' as she calls it.

"I told her, 'You're driving this bus,' meaning that she's in charge. Bad analogy. She immediately said, 'I wish I was still driving.' I changed gears quickly and said, 'Okay. Maybe it's not a bus. Let's say you're pushing this walker!' She laughed at that.

"She said she's enjoying the process, having things to think about, having some hope. She feels she's in charge of the decision, and that it's doable. She was in very good spirits when I left.

"We'll see where the Lord takes it from here."

⌒✹⌒

A friend once told me, "Love is actively seeking the very best for the other person." Lord, I understand now that I wasn't acting in love when we were looking into Klassen Manor. I was acting in my own best interest. I wanted Mom moved somewhere safe so I could share the responsibility of caring for her.

Here's what I know, but don't always remember: when I am invested in the outcome, I begin working in my own strength. When I work in my own strength, I'm not only pushing aside direction from the Holy Spirit. I'm also putting myself above you because I've decided how the situation should play out.

That's not love. That's serving myself at the expense of the person at the centre of the decision. Paul talks about it in 1 Corinthians 13 when he says we should exercise our gifts, but if we don't do it in love, we're nothing more than a clanging cymbal.

As soon as I believe someone needs to behave in a certain way so my vision can be fulfilled, it's a sure sign that I've gotten off track.

I wasn't at peace during the Klassen Manor planning. I was working hard to push my agenda on Mom, plotting and scheming and manipulating. This time, even during that difficult doctor's visit, I don't feel I have to control what's going to happen. I simply need to be present in the moment and support Mom to get through that event.

In a nutshell, I need to do the very best I can in any given situation, wholeheartedly as unto the Lord, and be willing to shift directions at a moment's notice, even if that means letting go of the current plan. The only way to achieve that is to invest all my love and energy into the moment, and have no investment in the outcome.

I believe fully understanding and walking in this truth is the way to achieve that mysterious peace that passes all understanding. Thank you, Lord, for being willing to take me through this lesson over and over again. Thank you for never giving up on me.

Decision Time

Two weeks have passed since I last called Mom. Each morning I ask, "Lord? Today?" and each morning I feel peace in waiting. This evening Lawrence phoned with an update. "I called Mother this afternoon to say hello. We talked about our visit to Whyte Hall last week when I was in town. She got my letter that described everything we saw. She read it back to me and we talked some more about it. Then she said, 'When is your sister going to do this?' I think she's been reading your notes and going through the information. I think she's ready to commit to the move."

"This is October 27th. If we take action now, she could be in for November," I said, a little stunned. *Could this really be happening?*

"Give her a call," Lawrence said. "I'll make myself available when you need me."

"I'll let you know," I told him. "Pray!"

"That I shall," my non-believing brother replied, getting into the spirit, so to speak. "Talk to you soon."

I closed my eyes. *Now, Lord?*

Peace.

I took a breath and dialed Mom's number.

"Good morning," I responded to her hello.

"Bobbi? Is it now? When are we were doing this. This…" There was silence for a moment, and then she said, "You'll have to talk because I don't have words."

"Are you talking about moving to Whyte Hall, Mom?"

"Have you and Rick finished moving?"

"No, Rick and I aren't moving," I reminded her. "But we've been talking about Rick and I helping you move to Whyte Hall. Have you thought more about that?"

"Well yes. Did those men get the money? Didn't they tell you?"

Money? Lord, help me understand. "Did someone come to your door asking for money?"

"Not the door. My bed is in the middle of the room. I heard them talking about it. One had an accent."

I remembered her habit of listening to the radio 24/7. I was pretty sure she was referring to the imaginary people she believed were moving around the house when she's sleeping. Perhaps she'd heard voices on a program about financial matters.

"No, Mom. No one from Whyte Hall was to come and ask for money. We only dealt with women there. Do you remember? One was the manager, Lauren, who gave us the application package. The other woman was the program director who took you and Lawrence around."

"So it's only a women's place?"

"We've only talked to women who work there," I clarified. "Have you thought more about moving in? Is that something you want to do?"

"Well, this is just too long. I've told myself that I have to give it a year. I was so surprised that they'll allow us to keep the house that long. And sometimes we give up too fast. So I have to give it a year and then decide."

"So you want to move to Whyte Hall and give it a year and see how it goes. Is that right?"

"Lawrence said he wanted to move his friends in there. I don't know how many." I ignored this strange comment. It seemed like a rabbit trail not worth exploring. Mom continued. "People just have to make that decision, don't they? I was thinking about the little silver boxes with flappers…"

My mind raced to decode, and the Lord didn't fail me. "You mean the mail boxes at Whyte Hall?"

"Yes! I was so surprised to see those. What a good idea. That's so smart."

"Mom, I think you're saying that it's time to jump in with both feet and see what happens. Is that right?"

"I've read over the notes and your brother's letter so many times." Trying to get Mom to say yes was proving impossible. Still, she was very agreeable.

Lord, can you give me an indication that this is definitely Mom's desire and not just mine?

With confidence I stated, "I'll call for an appointment tomorrow and we'll go and sign the papers. What do you think?"

"What time?"

"I'll let you know," I said, trying to contain my elation.

That sounds like a 'yes' to me! We're on our way, Lord. May you guide and direct me, and pull me back quick-fast if I start veering off course. Deal? Deal!

⁓∞⁓

I arrived at Mom's a half-hour before our meeting. She was waiting at the door with the same little brown Starbucks bag she had taken with her the Saturday she'd walked to Whyte Hall, ready to move in. The same clippings, letters, bills, cardboard, and advertisements were neatly tucked inside.

"I decided I should just take everything," she told me, holding it up.

"Wise."

"Then we won't have to slow things down to come back for anything," Mom added.

"Yes, it's easy to forget that one thing they're going to want," I agreed. "Let's see if the application is in there."

We spent the next ten minutes going through the bag, then the papers on her table, and a shoebox of new papers. Eventually we found the manila envelope I had labeled "Application for Whyte Hall" on her bedside table. With everything ready, we headed out.

"I'm going to go through the Rental Agreement with you, Nancy," the pleasant young manger explained. "We'll read each item and I'll need you to initial each page."

We sat at a round table in the empty dining room. Mom was almost vibrating with anticipation. As the discussion progressed, my amazement grew. My mother, who lives to find conspiracy around every corner, who sees the glass not only as half-empty but also as cracked and dirty, was thrilled with every aspect of the meeting.

Lauren reviewed the contract in detail. While Mom expressed pleasure at each rule, there were many items she clearly didn't grasp. Still, she initialed eight pages of information. I silently wondered how legal all this really was, given her limited understanding. It was a moot point, however. Mom had engaged my help, and in my view, all seemed to be in good order.

Each detail tickled Mom's fancy. "That's how you manage laundry? That's so intelligent," Mom proclaimed. "You take money ahead in case someone makes holes in the wall? It's about time people figured out how to do this. How smart." "Cleaning people just show up? Every week? And this is where you eat? How you manage all this, I don't know!"

Everything met with Mom's approval. Half an hour later the contract was signed, banking information had been taken, and we were ready to inspect the apartment.

"We have one vacancy on the main floor," Lauren explained. "It's through a very heavy fire door. You might have difficulty with that. The other is #416. You and your son looked at it a few weeks ago. Would you like to see that one again?"

Given Mom's earlier reticence about living "up in the air," I was pleasantly surprised when she replied with enthusiasm. "Isn't it amazing that you can live so high? But not all the way high at the top. This is better."

Whyte Hall has seven floors. It appeared the fourth level felt like a reasonable compromise to Mom. Lauren carried a clipboard with an inspection checklist attached.

"An inspection," Mom extolled. "What a smart idea. Finally people are thinking!" The three of us moved through the one-bedroom apartment, noting any scratches or bumps in the walls, checking the floors, the bathroom and tiny kitchenette. Mom expressed concern about using the microwave as she'd never owned one. I assured her we could teach her what she'd need to know. Mom tried every light switch, turned taps on and off, and peered out the window to the back alley.

"Isn't it lovely," she proclaimed.

Lauren handed Mom a new folder of papers. "We'll see you November second, then, Nancy. Here are the *Moving In* instructions. Be sure to time your arrival according to the directions. We'll see you soon."

Together we rode down in the elevator. Mom beamed at Lauren as she walked away. I turned Mom towards the entrance.

"Didn't that lady have a sparkle?" Mom said. "She had such a sparkle about her!"

"You really liked her, didn't you?"

I showed Mom how to push the exit button that opened the main doors. A resident with a walker was coming in. We stepped aside to make way.

Suddenly Mom leaped forward, practically accosting the woman. "Hello," she exclaimed, placing her hand on the walker bar. 'I'm moving in next week!'. The elderly woman was taken aback but was gracious nonetheless. She nodded and smiled, then quickly ducked out of our way.

Back in Mom's kitchen, I wrote out the details of the meeting. "Today we signed a Tenant Agreement, we set a moving date of November 2, and we arranged for automatic bank withdrawals for the rent. Bobbi will book a moving truck to arrive the afternoon of the second. Lawrence will come that day to help."

"So many things to think about," Mom said with a thrill in her voice.

"Good things," I added.

"Very good things!" Mom agreed.

⸎

Driving home, I felt as excited as Mom.

Only you, Lord, could work such a miracle in Mom's heart. Ever since I can remember, Mom has seen the world through negative, suspicious lenses. I know this is your handiwork because it's absolutely contrary to Mom's normal self. You are doing a wonderful work and I love that I get to watch it happen. May we keep moving forward in your perfect will.

What Could Go Wrong?

om and I sat at her kitchen table and conducted a final review of the documents from Whyte Hall, ready for the following Thursday. Suddenly Mom looked me straight in the eye, a startled expression on her face.

"I get so mad."

"You've said that before," I observed cautiously.

"I get mixed up. I don't know anything sometimes."

"It's hard for you, isn't it?"

"But you." Her expression softened. "You say just the right thing that brings me back. So I can think again. How do you do that?"

Lord, I want to tell her it's you who's doing this. Dealing with dementia is way beyond my ability. Only because of you can I manage to support Mom in ways that are helpful. But you won't let me speak. I feel I'm only allowed to tell Mom what you do for me in my own life, and even then, not very often. I'm allowed to show your love for her in practical ways, but nothing more. I see her responding. It's making an impression.

Lord, please let her understand that it's you she's seeing in me, and how much she needs you.

And Lawrence. When I told him Mom had decided to move to Whyte Hall of her own volition, he blew me away by saying, "This is the miracle you've been expecting, isn't it?"

Lord, you consistently surprise me, and confound me at the same time. You do amazing work through situations I'd eliminate in a heartbeat if I could. That would be why you're in charge and we're not. Your ways and your thoughts are so much higher than ours.

Mom and I turned back to the documents. I thought she was tracking with me but once again her mind shifted.

"You and your brother were awful!"

"We were?"

"Yes. You would scream and fight and make me crazy while I was trying to study. You were both hateful. Just hateful."

"Do you mean when we were in our teens and you went back to school?"

She sniffed.

"Did you think Lawrence and I were doing it on purpose, just to make it hard for you?"

"I know you were," she practically snarled. "You two knew exactly what you were doing."

I was quiet.

What a revelation, Lord. I don't recall fighting with Lawrence much back then, but if that's how Mom saw it, she must have felt we were trying to sabotage her plans. I was thirteen when she went to university to get an education degree. Her goal was to earn enough money so she could support herself and be able to leave my father. Her plans were secret, though. No one knew, not even her best friend Winnie until she actually bought the house she's moving out of next week. For six long years she secretly worked toward achieving her plan. Goodness. I never considered it from this perspective. No wonder she couldn't tell us to be quiet, demand that we help her by behaving. Her goal was to break up the family. She must have felt guilty, but determined nonetheless. It's impossible to live a lie and expect relationships to flourish. What a hopeless situation for all of us.

But now, today, Mom and I do have a relationship. Only you, Lord, could create the circumstance that would bring Mom and me together. Without you, I would have wanted nothing to do with a mother who hurt and rejected me. With you, I can understand what it means to honour my mother. When I look at her through your eyes, I see someone you love, someone you want to draw to yourself. If I can be your hands, then I know you'll bless me for that, even when I struggle to do your will. It's not wrong to be tempted, not wrong to be hesitant, not wrong to have an inner battle, as long as I take those thoughts captive and bring them to you.

Each time, you and I go a little further together. In the process I'm able to know and understand my mother and our relationship a little bit more.

Jesus, you really are amazing!

⸻❦⸻

Everything was in place. Today was the day. I sat watching the sunrise through my living room window and breathed deeply.

Okay, Lord. This is it. I'm off to Mom's for 10:00 a.m. No idea how things will play out, just that they will. Mom's fully on board and I have no fear she'll back out this time. The movers are confirmed to arrive at one. Whyte Hall rules state that moves must be completed between one and four-thirty pm. The elevator can't be used after four-thirty as the residents will be coming down for dinner. The one o'clock move time is critical, but we won't be taking much, so it should work out just right.

Nothing is packed yet. My car is filled with empty suitcases, bins and cloth grocery bags. My plan is to gather up everything Mom uses daily, pack the clothes from her two closets and her dresser, and put Sticky-Notes on the furniture we want the movers to take. I am placing Mom's ability to cope in your hands, Lord! Lawrence will arrive the same time as the movers. The forecast for today is ten degrees Celsius and dry. Tomorrow the weather gets cold and rainy. Thank you, Lord, for good weather!

⸻❦⸻

That evening I sent an email to the grandkids.

SUBJECT: The saga continues. Prayers needed!

"Grandma and I did great this morning. We packed everything and were ready for the movers by one. Lawrence arrived. We waited. No truck. We called. We waited. They called. They had the street and avenue reversed on the address so they were on the north side of the city. We waited some more. They finally arrived at three. The truck they brought was massive, big enough to move a whole house full of stuff. Grandma's little bit of furniture barely took up one corner.

"We loaded the truck and got to Whyte Hall around four and parked in front. The truck was too big to pull into the dropoff zone, so the movers parked illegally on the main street where no parking was allowed during rush hour. We took one load in and then it was four-thirty. Time to release the elevator for the residents to come down to dinner. The manager was firm. She said that the truck with all Grandma's stuff had to leave and couldn't come back until tomorrow.

"Oh my goodness!

"Lawrence went out with the movers and saw a commissioner preparing to ticket their truck. He quickly engaged the commissioner in conversation, giving the movers a chance to pull away and get the truck out of the restricted parking area. He caught up with them around the corner. Parking ticket averted.

"The movers called their boss. Since they were the ones who had confused the address, making them late, the boss told them to leave Grandma's stuff in the truck and bring it back to the yard. They will return to Whyte Hall at nine-thirty tomorrow morning.

"All Grandma's clothing, toiletries, bed and bedding are in the truck. With nowhere else to go, Lawrence and Grandma are here at our house, having a sleepover. We've just finished dinner. Donna from church brought over three frozen casseroles yesterday, saying people who are moving need meals! I didn't think we'd need them, but what a blessing to have something ready to warm up and eat!

"We're trying to relax and take it easy, but Grandma's very upset about staying here. She says she's putting us out, that we should find her a hotel and the movers should be made to pay. Please pray that she's able to settle down and relax and have a good night's sleep. I'll update everyone tomorrow!"

❦

I'd hoped that since Mom had felt so comfortable sleeping over that night a few months before, she would feel okay again, but that was not to be.

Rick, Lawrence, Mom, the dog and I made for a full house in our little bungalow. We made up a spare bed in the sewing room so Mom would be next to the bathroom. Lawrence took his bag to the bedroom downstairs.

Mom had nothing to sleep in. I was pretty sure a pair of my pyjama pants wouldn't suit her. They wouldn't fit her either. Taking advantage of Maggie's routine, I announced I was taking the dog for her walk. I grabbed my car keys, tossed Maggie into the back seat, and drove to the mall. There I picked up a nightgown and a robe. Returning home, I took Maggie for a short stroll around the block, then slipped in the back door, purchases tucked under my coat. Mom didn't notice, and I was able to lay out the nightgown and robe on her bed.

I found Mom sitting at the table, head in hand.

"I could use a cup of tea," I announced. "Would you like some, too?"

She looked at me listlessly but I was busy with my mental checklist. Bed made. Bed clothes ready. A mug of tea and canned milk, along with a few cookies on the table. I sighed in relief.

"Everything's in hand, Mom," I said brightly. "Just one more night…"

I spoke too soon.

"You never told me about any of this. You just signed the papers behind my back."

"You signed them, Mom. You initialed every page."

"Why won't you take me to my house? It's still there. I have the key."

"There's nothing there to sleep on. Your bed, your clothes and everything else are in the truck."

"I'll sleep on the floor."

"Oh Mom, you'd be so cold, and stiff and sore."

"What's wrong with you, keeping me here like this! Have I been kidnapped or something?"

I gave up trying to explain and let her vent.

After a half hour with me she caught Rick as he came out of the bathroom. "Rick, will you drive me home?"

"I can't do that, Nancy. There's nowhere for you to sleep there."

The two of them spent the next half hour sitting on her make-shift bed, discussing the situation.

Unable to sway Rick's resolve, Mom came out and tackled Lawrence. The topic had changed, however. I could tell she was very tired. Her words were much more confused.

"Who's paying your taxes? she demanded of Lawrence.

"I pay my taxes," he said, frowning.

"Then it shouldn't be you. It should be them."

"It should be who?"

"Those people in the night. They're still there at the house, aren't they? You've brought me here and now they get the whole house."

"No, Mother," Lawrence explained patiently. "Those are the voices on your radio. We've established that. Bedsides, your radio is in the moving truck. No one's at your house"

"You're lying. They're there and they're living for free. That's cheating. If they're living there at night they should be paying their part of the power and water bills. And the taxes."

I had to applaud her logic. "Well, that kind of makes sense," I agreed, "if people were really living in your house. But they're not. They're just voices on the radio."

"Then the radio station knows who they are. Who can I write to? Who is the radio station? I will write to them and tell them those people have to pay." Mom slumped down on the couch, her energy dwindling.

I nodded and said, "We could look into that tomorrow, after we've all had some sleep, okay?"

At that, she gave up. "I'm not happy about this. I'm not happy at all. But I guess I have no choice. You two are clearly running this show now."

"There's a nightgown on your bed, Mom, if you want to get changed."

"Why wouldn't there be," she huffed and marched down the hall.

Several minutes later she came out of the sewing room dressed in the soft pink nightie and knee-length terry robe. Purposefully she strode into our bedroom, came out and marched into the office, came out again and glared down the hallway. Finally she found the bathroom, the door next to the room where she was sleeping. When she came out, she was disoriented again. I wanted to help, but didn't think assistance would be welcomed. Finally she found her bedroom door, then turned and looked at me.

"Don't get old," she said. "Kill yourself early before they catch on." With that she closed the door.

⁂

Should we have taken her to a hotel, Lord? Or taken her back to her house to sleep in the spare bed in the basement? I didn't even ask you for direction, did I? Lawrence and I somehow decided the only option was to come back here.

Please help me remember to consult you as tomorrow unfolds.

What a wild day this turned into. I'm so glad you're in charge. May we all get a good night's sleep.

Sunshine and Smiles

A round 3:00 a.m. I was awakened by noise coming from the living room. Creeping down the hall, I found Mom sitting in the dark, in my rocking chair, bare legs stretched out on the footstool. Her small, frail appearance belied her determination as she vigorously rocked back and forth.

"Can't sleep?" I asked her.

"Who is that?" she asked, indicating the couch. "I think I sat on someone."

"Just a cushion," I said gently. "Would you like a blanket for your legs?" I lay a soft throw over her lap. "I'll turn the lamp on in your room so you can find your way back to bed."

Leaving her where she was, I crept back to my own bed, mindful that I had to work in the morning, then go and help settle Mom in the afternoon.

Lord, give me strength.

Mom was still in the rocker when I rose at 5:30. Rick was working the late shift, so we didn't disturb him. I called Lawrence to come and join us for breakfast.

"A bit early," he commented when he came upstairs, hair standing in salute on one side of his head.

"We didn't want you to miss breakfast," I said sweetly. "And I need to get to work early if I'm going to leave by one o'clock. My boss is being flexible, but there are things I need to get done."

"No problem," he answered agreeably as he poured some coffee.

Mom sat silently, snuggling her mug of tea between pale, blue-veined hands. I made toast and scrambled some eggs, wondering if any of us would eat them. I recalled that Mom never ate breakfast, and wasn't sure about Lawrence's habits. However, food was there if needed. I placed everything on the table in front of them, and hustled off to shower and dress.

Grabbing a piece of toast in one hand, and my purse in the other, I called goodbye. "See you at the Hall. I hope all goes well!"

Driving to work, I was secretly relieved that Lawrence was going to have to manage the rest of the move without me.

Lord, we're all so tired. Please help today go smoothly.

⤫

Lawrence called me at the office just before lunchtime. "Letting you know everything is in, the movers have been paid, and we're going down to the dining room in a few minutes."

"Well done," I commended him. "How did Mom do?"

"She stood around and watched, mostly. I told the guys where to put the furniture. Didn't bother asking her opinion. I figure we can move things later if they don't work where they are. You're coming up after lunch?"

"I should be there by one-thirty."

"See you then."

Could it be this easy, Lord? After yesterday's fiasco, is today unfolding gently? I guess I'll see for myself.

I found a spot on the street, taking careful note of the parking restrictions: *No Parking between 6:30 and 9:30, and 15:30 and 18:30. Tow Away Zone.*

That would be why the movers were nearly ticketed yesterday. This will make visits after work difficult. I'll have to scout out a different place to park. Today, I'll be sure to leave by three-thirty.

I buzzed Mom's apartment number from the call box in the entrance. Lawrence answered. "See Mom?" I heard him explaining.

"You push the number nine and that opens the door. Then Bobbi can come in."

"Isn't there a key?" Mom said in the distance as the buzzer released the door.

I wonder if she's going to be able to master letting people in? I'll have to rely on staff, or rule-breaking residents if she can't figure it out.

I smiled at a few seniors as I waited for the elevator. The receptionist placated a grumpy woman who was leaning on her walker by the desk. "I'll look into that in a few minutes, Mary. First I have to attend to this call."

Mary fumed and marched away, banging the walker on the floor as she rocked it angrily across the tile. *I guess Mom isn't the only person who gets angry.*

The elevator arrived. I stood back as two men, both with walkers, exited. One smiled at me. The other concentrated on maneuvering out the door. Pushing the very large button for the fourth floor, I waited patiently as the elevator rose.

Mom's suite was at the end of the hall. Wooden rails, as an aid to mobility, lined both walls. The door to #403 was propped open with a shoe. I could smell cigarette smoke wafting out from the gap. The manager had made it clear this was a No Smoking facility. I smiled to myself. *A little hard to enforce if someone has smoked all their life.*

Arriving at #416, I knocked firmly. Lawrence's voice came from the other side of the door. "That's Bobbi, Mom. You can open the door for her."

"How do you know that?"

"She buzzed up from the lobby. Remember? We dialed nine to let her in."

"We did?" Mom's voice sounded interested, and not at all stressed.

I waited patiently. The doorknob rattled and the door bumped back and forth. Finally it opened.

Mom greeted me with a brilliant smile. "You're my first visitor!" she exclaimed. "I have sun!" Mom drew me in and pointed to her favourite green chair, bathed in a warm sunbeam pouring through the south-facing window. I recalled Mom's house had no sunny windows. Like a kitten warming itself, she nestled into her arm chair and put her feet up on the footstool. It wobbled a bit.

"The leg came off," she said in a matter-of-fact tone. "Rick will fix that. You tell him."

"I'll be sure to do that," I assured her, settling myself on one of the kitchen chairs.

We visited for a while, shared tea and cookies. Mom gave me a tour and described each item of furniture and why it had been placed in its current position. "Lawrence says he's staying for a few days," she said. "He thinks that will be good."

"That's great, Mom. I have to go now to move the car before I get a ticket. I'll come to visit on the weekend. Okay?"

"I'll give you tea in my new house," Mom stated proudly. We hugged and I made my way home.

Nancy and Lawrence in her new apartment

⌒∞⌒

These months of helping Mom transition have given me a strong sense of déja vu, Lord. This morning I realized my mind was going back to those harrowing days when we helped Draya move from hospital to home, and then from our house to her own home. I was out of my depth every step of the way, dealing with the issues caused by her quadriplegia, managing her medical needs, addressing home care requirements, and trying to coordinate things I knew little about. Everyone was turning to me for direction, but I constantly felt out of control, and consequently like a failure. I panicked at every glitch, every unexpected turn. I was over-whelmed and exhausted.

Mom's transition had the same potential, as barriers and fears rose at the most unexpected times. This time, though, my response has been different.

During the past year as I've walked alongside Mom, you've given me a chance to learn what I didn't understand about walking with you when Draya had her accident. When Jesus is in charge, only two things are required:

Release the need to be in control.

Believe with complete faith that the Lord is going before and behind.

When we were helping Draya, I was consumed with planning and plotting and fretting about what might come next. The stress was over-whelming. What I understand now is that over-thinking, over-planning, and letting my anxiety rule had no impact on the outcome of Draya's circumstances. It did, however, have great impact on my emotional sta-bility, and on my husband, son and daughter. Friends, family, even the professionals would have helped if they could, but that wasn't possible. My turmoil was self-induced.

With hindsight, I can see you were going before and behind us in spite of me, just as you've been guiding and directing this journey with Mom. The difference is that then I thought I was responsible to control all the factors involved in Draya's care.

Some might call that arrogance. In truth, it was ignorance. I was unaware of all you could and would do if I simply backed off.

It's taken this journey with Mom for me to allow you the opportunity to prove your promises. You were knocking when I was helping Draya, but I wouldn't open the door. This time, when you knocked, I took a chance and let you in.

My only job in all of this has been to pray, trust, and walk alongside you, one day at a time.

As I dressed this morning I realized how stressed my brain has been lately. I tried to put my undies on over my pyjamas. I had Draya's jeans here to mend, and I tried to put them on instead of grabbing my own. I've made a few mix-ups like that in the last couple of days. In the past, such actions would have put me in a panic, thinking I was having a nervous breakdown. This time, though, I laughed instead. "Lord, can you believe I just did that?"

Why did settling Mom in a new living situation have to take so long? Why did we have to go through so many bumps to get Mom to Whyte Hall? I think I know one answer.

If Lawrence and I had had control over Mom's affairs, we would have bypassed this last year and moved her straight into a facility of our choice. Mom and I wouldn't have had the good moments we have had. I wouldn't have gained the insight and compassion that came as I learned more about Mom's past, and as I understood the struggles she was experiencing as a result of dementia. I would have lost this opportunity to lean on you, and to be equipped to serve you as I did by serving Mom.

Most of all, I wouldn't have been able to fully practice the peace that comes only from you. May I continue to grow according to the lessons you deem necessary in my life. May you be revealed through me and beyond me as this journey continues.

I place Mom and her new home fully in your hands, Lord. One day, this day, is all I can live. The past is finished. Tomorrow is yours.

You have searched me, Lord,
  and you know me.
You know when I sit and when I rise;
  you perceive my thoughts from afar.
You discern my going out and my lying down;
  you are familiar with all my ways.
Before a word is on my tongue
  you, Lord, know it completely.
You hem me in behind and before,
  and you lay your hand upon me.
Such knowledge is too wonderful for me,
  too lofty for me to attain.
Where can I go from your Spirit?
Where can I flee from your presence?
If I go up to the heavens, you are there;
if I make my bed in the depths, you are there.
If I rise on the wings of the dawn,
if I settle on the far side of the sea,
  even there your hand will guide me,
  your right hand will hold me fast.
If I say, "Surely the darkness will hide me
  and the light become night around me,"
  even the darkness will not be dark to you;
  the night will shine like the day,
  for darkness is as light to you.
For you created my inmost being;
  you knit me together in my mother's womb.
I praise you because I am fearfully and wonderfully made;
  your works are wonderful,
I know that full well.
My frame was not hidden from you
  when I was made in the secret place,
  when I was woven together in the depths of the earth.

Your eyes saw my unformed body;
all the days ordained for me were written in your book
before one of them came to be.
How precious to me are your thoughts, God!
How vast is the sum of them!
Were I to count them,
they would outnumber the grains of sand...

—Psalm 139:1-18

About the Author

Bobbi's experience with caregiving has spanned several seasons. In her early years, she worked with children who had been abused and neglected, as well as those with physical disabilities. Later, her daughter suffered a catastrophic injury and was left a quadriplegic. Bobbi and her husband worked as a team to care for their daughter, at the same time nurturing and supporting a growing son with Tourette Syndrome.

Writing and story have long been Bobbi's bridge for processing and sharing her questions, experiences, and learning. When her idea to write *The Reluctant Caregiver* took shape, Bobbi took part in writers' conferences and joined several writing groups, one of which culminated in the publishing of the writing group's anthology, *Telling Truths: Storying Motherhood*. Other publications include pieces in industry newsletters, Alberta Views, and FellowScript Magazine.

With the publication of *The Reluctant Caregiver*, Bobbi is moving on to new projects, one of which will be the sequel to her mother's story. In the meantime, Bobbi enjoys opportunities as a presenter and workshop leader, particularly in areas of caregiving. As Communications Coordinator for an Edmonton, Alberta, Human Services group, Bobbi continues to learn, encourage, and share information to support others on their journeys of healing and growth.

In addition to her careers, Bobbi serves as treasurer for InScribe Christian Writers' Fellowship and as chair of her church's Board of Directors.

Rick and Bobbi have been married over thirty years. Their adult children are successfully launched and Bobbi is enjoying a new, quieter season in her life. She is eager to share how Jesus brought her to terms with her past and led her to a present filled with peace and joy.

Bobbi Junior thoughtfully, clearly, and often humorously explores the topic of caregiving, and many others, on her blog. Visit her website at www.bobbijunior.com and contact her there. She welcomes your e-mails and stories of your own journey.